ELEGANT

WEDDINGS

THE CEREMONY ❧ THE RECEPTION ❧ THE CLOTHES

EDITED BY
JENS CHRISTIANSEN

PHOTOGRAPHY:
SANDRA BIRGERSDOTTER
LINDA BROSTRÖM

TRANSLATED BY
VERONICA CHOICE

SKYHORSE PUBLISHING

CONGRATULATIONS!

IF YOU'RE READING this book, it's very likely that you are soon to be married. Congratulations! You have taken the first big step in your lives together. In this book, you will find advice on how to plan your wedding to make it that special day you both are dreaming about. This book is intended as both a guide and a source of inspiration; it offers the wisdom we have acquired over the years through our work at Sweden's magazine *Allt om Bröllop (All About Weddings)*. The book highlights many of the questions our editors frequently receive regarding how to go about doing things, clarifications of all the details a wedding entails, and various traditions, as well as their origins. Please read the book and make use of our knowledge, but do feel free to pick and choose within our guide to make sure this day is customized to your wants. It is, after all, your own special day.

This book has been compiled by my hands, but it is also a work of love from our complete editorial staff here at the magazine. Contributing authors are Anna Fürst, Josefine Franking, Sara Kvarnström, Tommy Ditz, and myself, Jens Christiansen. Photographs are courtesy of Linda Broström and Sandra Birgersdotter.

Jens Christiansen

11 Steps to a Successful Wedding

1. WHERE, WHEN, AND HOW DO YOU WANT TO GET MARRIED?

The first step is to choose where, when, and how you want to get married so you can decide on a date. If you plan ahead of time, it is less likely that you'll run into obstacles such as booked churches or reception venues or that your guests will already have other plans. This is also a good time to start thinking about which friends and family members you would like to include in your wedding party. Read the sections *Find the Best Reception Hall* (page 183) and *Key People for the Wedding* (page 47).

2. SETTING YOUR BUDGET

There are two of you getting married and therefore it's important for you both to sit down to discuss your expectations and any other concerns you may have. How much money do you want to spend? How much can you afford to spend? It's easy for the costs to add up if they are not taken into account beforehand. Pay close attention to expenses by using our budget list (page 228).

3. NOTIFYING YOUR GUESTS

Of course you want the whole world to know you are getting married! Clear and detailed information about your special day is the key to making your wedding go as smoothly as possible. Complete the guest list (page 232) and read about how best to go about inviting all your loved ones (page 51), how to thank them afterward (page 62), and how to manage everything in between in style.

4. CREATING YOUR WISH LIST

Many guests will want to celebrate your love and happiness by bringing gifts. It is an important part of the wedding, which can cause unwanted complications both for you as a couple as well as your guests if it is not managed properly. Read our suggestions about what to wish for and information on how to communicate your wishes in the best way (pages 55–57).

5. CHOOSING THE RIGHT PHOTOGRAPHER

The wedding photos will display your memories for life. Think about what kind of photography you want and then search for a photographer who specializes in exactly that. Some photographers get booked well in

advance, and both style and cost may vary. Read about what to consider and what not to forget to ensure that your wedding day photography will be perfect (pages 87–90).

6. CREATING THE PERFECT WEDDING LOOK

Of course you want to look the most beautiful you can on your wedding day, so you will find a whole chapter on how to create the perfect wedding look for both bride (pages 97–143) and groom (pages 145–169). There is also plenty of useful information about dress codes (pages 52–53).

7. FINDING THE RIGHT WEDDING BANDS

The rings symbolize your undying love for one another and hopefully you will continue to wear them every day for the rest of your lives. Perhaps you want custom-made rings to ensure that they are truly unique. Read about how to find the perfect rings (pages 171–177) and other glamorous items to accent your wedding day.

8. FLOWERS TO BRIGHTEN UP THE WEDDING DAY

The flowers might not be an essential part of your wedding planning, but they are often more important than you might think for setting the atmosphere of your wedding. They help bring to life your vision and can turn even the simplest room into a gorgeous reception hall. Find suggestions, inspiration, and information about what kinds of flowers are in season during your wedding (pages 75–85).

9. ORGANIZING THE SEATING CHART

When all of your guests have responded to your invitation, it's time to decide where everyone should be seated during the reception dinner. It's impossible to make everyone happy, but there are some tricks for success (pages 186–187).

10. BOOKING THE BEST HONEYMOON TRIP

After the wedding, it is important to spend some precious alone time with each other. Read about how to find the hottest destinations and what to consider when booking a honeymoon trip (pages 93–95).

11. MANAGING YOUR CHECKLIST

The best way to manage the wedding plans is to use the checklist at the back of this book (pages 226–227). Check off completed tasks as you go along and keep track of what needs to be done at various stages of planning.

THE CEREMONY

Love for as Long as You Both Shall Live

Some people prefer to marry in secret, some prefer a civil ceremony during their lunch break, and others dream of a lavish affair with an equally spectacular reception to follow. No matter what kind of wedding you choose, this day is all about love, and during the ceremony you will have a chance to express your feelings for one another.

The most common is a traditional church wedding or a civil ceremony at the courthouse with a reception afterward for friends and family. Lately, however, destination weddings have become more and more popular, though that can bring additional challenges.

There is no right or wrong when choosing how you want to get married— the most important thing is to do what's right for you. In this chapter, you will find some of the most commonly used nuptials and what you should keep in mind.

ON YOUR SPECIAL DAY

YOU HAVE PREPARED for, longed for, and dreamed about it—and now, your special day is finally here. When you wake up on this day, you will almost certainly have butterflies in your stomach. This is when the preparations truly begin.

The bride often takes a few hours to get ready, with both hair and makeup on the to-do list. Together with her bridesmaids, she will enjoy some delicious champagne and perhaps some snacks as they all prepare themselves for the occasion. The groom usually takes this time to get dressed and spend some memorable moments with his groomsmen.

Some couples choose to see each other before the ceremony to take wedding pictures, while others prefer to not see one another until the ceremony itself. This first, precious moment when you lay eyes on each other in full wedding attire is truly magical. Cherish this special moment to the fullest!

Even though part of your wedding day has already passed, it probably won't be until the ceremony that you will realize the significance of the moment. Some get emotional to the point of tears, while others can't stop laughing. Everyone gets emotional during the nuptials. After you have said your "I dos" and have been declared husband and wife, the nervousness usually dissipates. Now it's time to celebrate!

After your guests have tossed the ceremonial rice over you, you can expect an overflow of congratulations from everyone who has shared your special moment. It's now time for the guests to leave for the reception hall while you use the opportunity to take photographs. The elation you feel will shine in each photo. This is also a great opportunity to share some first private moments as husband and wife.

When you reach the reception hall, you will be greeted by a toast, and afterward it's time for dinner. The heartfelt and funny speeches will likely distract you from fully enjoying the delicious food, but in this moment, does it really matter? Some small snafus may arise during the day, or something won't happen exactly as you had planned, but just relax and embrace the day!

The first dance and the slicing of the wedding cake ends the day's traditions, and then you can dance the night away. You are sure to fall into bed in the wee hours of the morning after a night of celebrations, and hopefully you will both have experienced one of the best days of your lives together. One thing is certain: the day will move faster than you anticipated. Make sure you enjoy every moment of this special day—it's what you have been longing for during all the steps of the planning process.

Bubbles and flower petals are beautiful and fun alternatives to the traditional rice tossing.

HOW DOES IT WORK
AND WHAT DO WE HAVE TO DO?

CIVIL CEREMONY OR A CHURCH WEDDING—which is more appropriate for you? One of the first steps in planning a wedding is usually to choose the kind of ceremony you both prefer. There are other ways to conduct a wedding ceremony, but the most common ones are either the civil ceremony at city hall or the traditional church wedding. A church wedding does not necessarily have to take place in a church, just as a civil ceremony does not have to take place at city hall. Perhaps you would like to take your vows before a priest beside ocean cliffs or maybe have a civil ceremony in your own backyard. Whatever you choose, it is important to remember that even if you want to take your vows before a priest outside the confines of a church, it may still be considered a religious ceremony and the ceremony may not be allowed to change.

A marriage must be performed by an officiator qualified by the state, such as a priest, minister, or rabbi, or in the case of a civil ceremony, a mayor, judge, justice of the peace, or county clerk. In many cases, that person will charge a fee for his/her services. The officiating party can also request reimbursement for travel expenses if the ceremony is held outside the congregational church.

Marriage Equality

Though much of the United States does not yet recognize gay marriage, more and more states have been adopting legislation to legalize it. Check what the laws are in your state, and, if necessary, get married out of state. Keep up to date on current gay marriage laws on the Human Rights Campaign website *www.hrc.org*.

In the United States, gay marriage is still controversial, though more and more states are legalizing it.

Marriage License

No matter what kind of ceremony you decide on, all couples must apply for a marriage license. The cost of the license will vary from state to state, generally costing less than $100. Most states require individuals below the age of eighteen to have parental consent to be married. If two parties are related or already married to another party, they are not eligible to be married. Many states require a waiting period between the time the license is issued and the ceremony itself. In most states the marriage license is valid for thirty to ninety days, depending on the state. Nevada gives one full year. In all states the license must be valid during the ceremony.

Keep in mind that in most states the marriage license is only valid for thirty to ninety days. If you need more time than that, you will have to reapply for a new license.

Marriage Certificate

When your application for a marriage license has been approved, you will receive a marriage license from the county clerk's office. The person who conducts your ceremony will then fill out all the necessary information after the ceremony and will send it back to the county clerk's office. Not until this procedure has taken place is the marriage considered legally valid. After receiving the marriage license signed by the bride and groom, witnesses, and the officiator, the county clerk's office will send a certified copy of the license and a marriage certificate to you. It will generally arrive in a few weeks.

A New Last Name

If you want to change your name as a result of your wedding, on the application you will fill out which last name you choose, and you will have the opportunity to keep your name or just add your partner's name. If you do not apply for a new last name, you will automatically keep your individual last names, but you still have the option to change your name at a later date.

Witnesses

Whether you marry in a civil ceremony or in a church, there always need to be one or two witnesses, depending on the state, present at the ceremony who are eighteen years of age or older. The wedding is not binding if there are no witnesses. If you cannot find any personal witnesses, there are always staff members on hand who are more than happy to serve.

CHURCH CEREMONY

IF A COUPLE WANTS TO BE MARRIED in a denominational church, they should devote considerable time to familiarizing themselves with the special traditions and ceremonies of marriage in their religion. So how do you go about having a church wedding if you are a member, but not necessarily very religious? Can you change what is said during the nuptials?

First of all, it is important to remember that depending on the denomination, a church wedding will take place during a service where the couple is blessed by God. This means that it is not only a ceremony, but also a service in itself. Therefore, for some churches, it will be impossible to remove any mandatory parts that are included in a church ceremony. However, this is not the case for all denominations or churches, so speak with your priest, minister, or rabbi to see what is allowed.

Of course, even if your church is very strict, there are always ways to make the ceremony more personal, and it's important to get involved in these steps. You can have a lot of influence over the ceremony by meeting with the priest, minister, or rabbi before your wedding day. This is not mandatory, but it's a good opportunity to go over the practicalities while letting the priest get to know the two of you better. It is then easier for him or her to personalize the ceremony so it reflects the two of you. It also gives you a chance to get to know the priest, minister, or rabbi who will conduct your nuptials, and if the chemistry between you and the priest is not what you want, you can easily request another person to conduct your ceremony. It is your day, after all!

During the wedding discussion you will review everything from what happens during the ceremony to the order of the hymns that will be included. Feel free to discuss with your priest, minister, or rabbi any additional wishes you may have in regards to readings, songs, or music during the ceremony.

There are also opportunities to get married outside or at a location other than the church. Contact your congregation to find out more about your options.

Wedding Vows

Don't forget to decorate the church to make it more personal.

Although in some churches you cannot ask your priest to tone down the religious content, as it would be wrong for the priest to do so, there are always opportunities to make the ceremony special to you. Many people don't consider the possibility of writing their own vows, thereby making the ceremony more personal. If you choose to write your own vows, it is important to write them well ahead of time so what you read during the ceremony is exactly the same as what you have given the priest, minister, or rabbi.

Think about what you want to do, because this can be a nervous part for some and, as a wedding can be stressful in itself, the personalized vows may seem like just an added stress. One option is to write personal vows, but not to read them out loud during the ceremony. The priest will then take your vows and hand them over to you at the same time as your marriage certificate.

If you choose to write your own vows for a church wedding, you should consult your clergy person, as each religion has it own set of guidelines for what is appropriate. First and foremost, you should make it clear that you are marrying for love and not, for example, because of the other partner's money. Usually, wedding vows read something like this:

"I hereby take thee as my lawful wedded wife to have and to hold from this day forward, for better and for worse, for richer and for poorer, in sickness and in health, to love, honor, and cherish, 'til death do us part."

Some people find these words to be dated and therefore choose to write their own vows. They can sound something like this:

"I promise that pride will not destroy our love and I promise to always try even when life is difficult. I will help you when you need help, and will turn to you when I need help. With you I want to share sorrow, joy, and old age."

After the wedding vows, the priest or minister will ask you "do you . . . take this . . ." and this is when you both will have to say "I do" for the marriage to be legally valid. The priest will then acknowledge you as a lawfully wedded couple.

If you write your own vows, be sure to practice reading them ahead of time. When the time comes to read them during the ceremony it is easy to get nervous.

CIVIL CEREMONY

A CIVIL CEREMONY is just as legally binding as a church ceremony, but without the religious elements. Many people who choose to marry in a civil ceremony do so because of their beliefs, but it can also be a good solution for when the bride and groom are of different religions.

A common misconception is that a civil ceremony is always short and without emotion. The standard civil ceremony doesn't last more than a minute or so, but there are often options to add music or read poetry. The civil ceremony doesn't have the same rules as some church ceremonies do and can often be shaped after one's own preference. You can, for example, get married outside on a cliff by the ocean with your closest family and friends or even at a reception hall surrounded by all your loved ones.

The marriage ceremony can take place practically anywhere you like, and it is common to hold it city hall. Anyone can apply at the county clerk's office for permission to perform ceremonies, but usually these officials are appointed by recommendation of the county. Contact the county clerk's office to get a list of officiating parties in your area. If you choose to get married at city hall in a larger city, it may not be possible to choose who will perform the ceremony, as they might just assign you whomever is on duty that day.

Just as with a church ceremony, you will need a marriage license (see page 22), and if nothing has been stated otherwise, you will bring this license with you to the ceremony. You can choose to bring your own witnesses or have the staff on site act as your witnesses.

Rings are not required, but many couples choose to exchange rings anyway since the symbolism of the rings is so significant. Neither is there a requirement for wedding vows, so if you don't want to write your own you don't have to, but there is the option to do so if you would like to.

There are also many possibilities to make a civil ceremony into a festive occasion equal to a church wedding. Speak to your wedding officiator ahead of time to hear what options are available for you. You can find more information on the city hall website.

OTHER RELIGIOUS CEREMONIES

According to law, the wedding officiator has to be certified. If you cannot find such an officiator within your community, you will have to wed in a civil ceremony to make the marriage legally binding. Check with your community board to hear if they have a certified officiator.

MUSIC DURING THE CEREMONY

MUSIC IS A NATURAL PART of the church ceremony, whether you choose to marry within the church or if you get married on the beach before a priest. At a church, the cantor manages most of the music, but you can personalize it nonetheless. Perhaps you have talented friends who can sing and would like to perform; this is a great way to make the ceremony more intimate. If you have any personal wishes as to what the cantor should play, you should set up an appointment with him or her well ahead of time to express your wishes.

Entrance and exit music are always included during a traditional church ceremony, along with at least two hymns. The entrance music, also known as the wedding march, is played when the bride walks up to the altar, and the exit music is played when the bride and groom walk out of the church together as the ceremony ends.

If you are planning to get married in a civil ceremony, you will have to provide any potential music. If you get married at another location, for example city hall, it is usually not a problem to frame the ceremony with music. It is, however, not always possible to have live music if the ceremony is held at city hall. Ask what applies to your community specifically.

Entrance and Exit Music

The cantor will often select grand pieces as the entrance and exit music, and there are plenty of wedding marches to choose from. The most popular processional in the United States is the *Bridal Chorus* from Richard Wagner's *Lohengrin*. In Western services, the preferred recessional is Felix Mendelsson's *Wedding March* from *A Midsummer Night's Dream*. However, there are many other classical pieces to choose from. Here are a few:

Bridal Chorus from *Lohengrin* – Richard Wagner
Wedding March from *A Midsummer Night's Dream* – Felix Mendelssohn
Prince of Denmark's March – Jeremiah Clarke
Canon in D Major – Johann Pachelbel
Trumpet Tune – Henry Purcell
Rondeau – Jean-Joseph Mouret
Hornpipe from *Water Music* – George Frideric Handel
Grand March from *Aida* – Guiseppe Verdi

⫸ You can choose whatever pieces you like as entrance and exit music. It doesn't have to be a march; however, you may want to seek advice from your cantor and priest regarding your choice of music.

Hymns

The hymns played during a church wedding can certainly be about love between people and between God and man. It is also popular to choose a seasonal hymn, for example a summertime hymn or a Christmas hymn. Here are some favorites:

Hymn 82 – *God, be merciful on these two*
Hymn 84 – *We lift our hearts*
Hymn 85 – *As man and woman joyous together*
Hymn 199 – *Blooming times are coming*
Hymn 200 – *In this lovely summer time*
Hymn 201 – *A kind and rich green*
Hymn 289 – *God's love is as the beach*
Hymn 297 – *Wonderful is the earth*
Hymn 411 – *God is considerate to our kind*
Hymn 751 – *Oh how the world is wonderful*
Hymn 754 – *When the day is filled with birdsong*
Hymn 791 – *You do know that you are valued*
Hymn 903 – *I believe that God is love*

Love Songs

Perhaps you have a friend or a relative who wants to do a solo or a musical number during the ceremony. A list of great love songs could end up being infinite, so here is a quick selection.

The Wedding Song – Paul Stookey
When I Fall in Love – Nat King Cole
We've Only Just Begun – The Carpenters
Wonderful World – Louis Armstrong
I Can't Help Falling in Love with You – Elvis Presley
You Are So Beautiful – Joe Cocker
All I Ask of You from *Phantom of the Opera* – Andrew Lloyd Webber
At Last – Etta James

> ⫸ Wedding music is more than just entrance and exit music. Don't forget the guests will want something to dance to. Read more about this on page 215.
>
> ⫸ Do you both have a special song that elicits happy memories of your relationship? Play it at your wedding to make your day even more personal.

Instrumental Music

Instrumental music gives time for reflection and sets the mood for the ceremony. The cantor or someone else with musical knowledge can surely help you with suggestions and ideas. It is extra special if you have a friend who can play something during the ceremony.

Ave Maria (D 389) – Franz Schubert
Preludium in S Major – Johan Sebastian Bach
Prelude No 1 – Johan Sebastian Bach
Air on a string – Johan Sebastian Bach
The Swan – Camille Saint-Saëns
Love song – Johan Sebastian Bach
Canon in D Major – Johann Pachelbel
Ave Maria – Charles Gounod

≫ Seek advice from your cantor regarding hymns and music.

≫ Depending on the church, hymns may be required for church weddings. You are, however, free to choose all other music.

Poetry

It is quite common for someone to read poetry during the ceremony, and you may even want to print a poem on the wedding program. If you prefer not to write your own words for the vows there are many suitable poems to choose from.

"Sonnet 116" – William Shakespeare
"Sonnet 18" – William Shakespeare
"The Good-Morrow" – John Donne
"How Do I Love Thee" – Elizabeth Barrett Browning
"Marriage" – Mary Weston Fordham
"Love's Philosophy" – Percy Bysshe Shelley
"My Love" – Linda Lee Elrod
"Wedding Prayer" – Robert Lewis Stevenson
"A Dedication to My Wife" – T. S. Eliot
"To My Dear and Loving Husband" – Anne Bradstreet
"Hope Is the Thing with Feathers" – Emily Dickinson
"Fidelity" – D. H. Lawrence
"She Walks in Beauty" – Lord Byron
"The Prophet" – Kahlil Gibran

DESTINATION WEDDINGS

DO YOU DREAM OF getting married barefoot on a beach in the Caribbean or saying "I do" at the top of the Eiffel Tower? Whether you want to marry in secret in another country or you want a spectacular wedding on the Riviera, there are always things to consider beforehand. If you invite a hundred guests to a vineyard in Toscana, it is important to consider if you should pay for the guests' travel expenses or if you should only invite the ones who can afford such an affair. If you choose to elope abroad, it is a good idea to have a symbolic ceremony at home afterward so your loved ones can have a chance to celebrate you.

The first thing to do is to choose which country you want to get married in since different countries have different rules for getting married. Contact the State Department or the embassy to find out what rules apply to the country of your choice. There are many wedding alternatives when marrying outside the United States. The US embassy and consulate personnel cannot perform marriages in foreign countries. There are a lot of rules that have to be followed, so ask for advice from the embassy of the country where you plan to get married and the US Embassy before you leave. Information about foreign churches and city halls can be found on every country's government home page.

If you want to get married abroad and need to know if your marriage will be recognized in the United States and what documentation may be needed, contact your state's Office of the Attorney General.

Did you know it's possible to get married at the airport chapel? Many choose this option just before traveling and then have a personal ceremony on a beach somewhere.

Do you dream of getting married on a desert island surrounded by the turquoise ocean? Check carefully what rules apply before you make your decision. It can be more complicated than you think.

THINGS TO CONSIDER
IF YOU WANT TO GET MARRIED ABROAD

≫ If either of you is divorced or is a widow or widower, many countries require that the documents certifying the end of any previous marriages (such as death or divorce certificates) be submitted, translated into the local language, and authenticated.

≫ Bring valid identification papers, copies of valid passports, and documents regarding impediments to marriage, as listed above.

≫ In certain countries you are required to have a marriage license to prove that you have the right to marry. In certain cases you might have to apply on-site. To obtain such a license you will have to show a marriage license issued in the United States.

≫ Marriage certificates are provided by the local church or embassy after the wedding ceremony.

LEGAL ASPECTS

LAWS COVERING prenuptial agreements, inheritance, and divorce vary from state to state, so you should familiarize yourself with the laws of the state in which you are to marry well in advance of the wedding. Discuss where you stand on these and similar issues to avoid any uncomfortable surprises.

Marriage involves some legal changes that are important to know about. The rules—which are there primarily to protect both parties and any potential children—mean that you as a married couple have both more protection and more obligations toward one another.

One of the biggest differences in comparison to a domestic partnership is that domestic partners do not have obligations toward one another. Though it is legally easier to break up a domestic partnership, you are not offered the same protection that comes with marriage, and you would not necessarily be entitled to any of the other partner's property. Married couples, however, may be entitled to alimony, child support, and distribution of property—money, personal items, real estate, and household goods, whether they were acquired before, during, or after the marriage. In the case of divorce, in most states a divorce must be certified by a court of law. If you would like to make provision for division of property during a separation, it is important to create a prenuptial agreement with the help of your lawyer. In most states, the prenup must be executed and acknowledged before a notary. A prenuptial agreement must be completed before marriage in order to be valid; alternately, after the marriage has taken place you can create a post-nuptial agreement.

In the worst-case scenario—at the death of a spouse—the remaining spouse has more protection than a domestic partner. In simple terms, this means that the living party inherits all of the spouse's property, including life insurance. If there are children from a previous marriage, they have the right to their legal share, while children within the marriage will only inherit from the parent who is still alive. By writing a will you can, of course, stipulate who will receive what.

Even though many things change during the course of a marriage, depending on which state you live in you are still considered separate individuals legally. In most states, this means that you are not automatically responsible for your partner's potential loans and debts. The indebted partner can therefore not request that you take part in paying off any debts incurred by him or her. The indebted party does, however, have the right to deduct his or her debt from the assets during a separation of property. Discuss where you stand on this issue and similar issues to avoid any surprises.

In most states, the prenup must be executed and acknowledged before a notary.

PLANNING

A Big and Exciting Project

Planning your wedding is exciting, but it can also feel like an enormous and overwhelming task. There are many pieces that have to fall into place, and you can't do it over again if anything goes wrong. But with a well-laid plan, your wedding will be as wonderful as you have dreamed.

Six months before the wedding is a good time to start planning the details. Sit down and talk about your expectations and create a list of priorities, writing down what is most important to you.

WHEN, WHERE, AND HOW?

THE FIRST PART of planning should focus on when and where the wedding will be held. Each season has its own special charm, although the summer is still the most common time for weddings. If you want a summer wedding, you should make sure to book your venues well ahead of time. If possible, you should try to book the venue close to a year in advance. Popular churches are usually booked solid long in advance and are especially popular on certain dates, for example, on days with a special number such as 11/12/13. Try to avoid big holidays such as Valentine's Day, when many have their weddings planned. If you're planning a summer wedding it's especially important to send out your invitations early since many people will be away on vacation during that time.

Winter weddings are not as common as summer weddings, so there are many advantages to getting married during this season. Reception halls, ceremony venues, and catering companies are more likely to be available, and during the low season it's often possible to get reduced rates. On the other hand, the flowers and decorations for a winter wedding may cost more due to limited supplies.

When you've decided on a date and location, it is time for the both of you to discuss your visions and expectations for the wedding. Are they the same or do you and your partner want different things? How much money you are willing to spend and who you want to invite are important things to discuss. Another question is how will you divide the planning so that both of you take part in the preparations? This is a question that is often overlooked and can create unnecessary frustration later on. There may be certain areas that are better suited to either of you.

One option that is common for those planning a large wedding or who are short on time is to hire a wedding planner. A wedding planner is a person who will take your vision and make it come to life while taking over most of the wedding preparations. For most couples, however, the planning is something fun and important that they prefer to do together.

The vast majority of weddings take place between May and August. A wedding during other months can be cheaper since fewer venues are booked.

PREPARATIONS FOR THE WEDDING

To make preparations easier, it is a good idea to make a schedule for when various tasks should be completed. On page 226 you can find a checklist to help you keep track of all the details and know when they should be completed.

BUDGET

KEEP AN EYE ON THE BUDGET

》 Remember to budget for all the flowers—not just bridal bouquet.

》 Find out if there is a season for the flowers you want; trying to special order out of season flowers can really break your budget.

》 Use the budget list on page 228 to keep track of costs.

》 Avoid borrowing money to pay for your wedding.

HOW MUCH WILL THE WEDDING cost? Well, how much do you want to spend? In earlier times, the bride's parents paid for the wedding, but if they haven't offered to do so, you shouldn't count on this tradition. After all, you will have to maintain good relations with your parents and your in-laws even after the wedding.

If you're paying for your own wedding, it is important to keep track of expenses. This is usually the most sensitive part of the planning, so make sure both of you are in agreement from the get-go. Do you want the same thing? A large and extravagant wedding or a small and intimate affair? Do you want to throw a big party with plenty of delicious food, good wine, and an open bar during the whole evening? Do you want live music or a DJ?

A wedding can be as small or as lavish as you choose, and it is important to take your time to think about what you both want so you are in agreement. You probably won't be able to afford everything, so you'll need to decide how much it should cost and then go over the various costs to make the most of your money.

Even though it can be tempting to borrow money for the wedding, be sure to really think twice about doing that. An important day such as your wedding day should not leave a sour aftertaste because of an expensive payment plan. Rather, save up some money for the wedding and start your life together off with a blank slate!

The average wedding costs between nineteen thousand and thirty thousand dollars, but of course it can be done with a lot less or a lot more. If you still want to serve a three-course meal, one option for those with a limited budget is to require your guests to pay a cover charge. However, if you do, it is customary not to expect any wedding presents.

To facilitate your planning, use the budget list on page 228. Fill out your anticipated costs and then the actual costs for everything as you go along.

If you are planning to take a helicopter to and from church, it's a good idea to create a very detailed budget early on.

KEY PEOPLE FOR THE WEDDING

RECEIVING HELP FROM OTHERS with your wedding is a priceless gift. If you are planning a big wedding, you should accept all the help you can get. The wedding party can be especially supportive if you start engaging them early in the planning process. It's also a lot of fun to plan your big day with your best friends. Friends and relatives also will usually feel honored to play an important role in your wedding day. But who does what and what can you expect from each and every person on your big day?

> ⋙ Talk about your expectations with the appointed key people for the wedding and what their tasks will be.

Host and Hostess

For every party there is always a host, and when it comes to weddings it is the host and hostess who invite the guests to the party. Traditionally it is supposed to be the parents of the bride who take on these roles, but these days, parents rarely pay for the wedding and therefore you can choose anyone you want for these roles. The host and hostess welcome the guests and make the first toast and speeches. They are responsible for making sure all the little details fall into place and are also the ones who answer any questions about the bridal registry.

Toastmaster

The person who has been designated by the bride and groom to organize the speeches is called the toastmaster or toast madame. In the United States, the role of toastmaster may also be performed by the Master of Ceremonies (MC), and it's not uncommon for couples to hire a professional to serve this function. In some instances, the wedding planner will even serve as the Master of Ceremonies or toastmaster. His or her task is to coordinate with the kitchen to make sure that the food is served in coordination with the speeches so everything flows nicely throughout the dinner. It is a good idea to write down the name and number of the toastmaster on the invitations so the guests will know who to contact if they would like to make a speech.

> ⋙ Keep track of the number of speeches and how long they will last. Instruct your toastmaster not to allow too many speeches or to let them last too long.

The toastmaster is not meant to be in the spotlight or to entertain the guests, which will often happen, but it's best if the toastmaster is not a shy person. Read more about how your toastmaster can succeed at the party on page 197.

Maid of Honor

The term "maid of honor" originally referred to the virgin attendant to the queen. Today, she is often a sister, female relative, or close friend of the bride. Her most important task is to offer support during the planning process and on the day of the wedding, and she is the one to organize the bridal shower and bachelorette party.

The maid of honor and the best man usually stand next to the bride and groom during the wedding ceremony. During the ceremony, she may hold the wedding bouquet as well as the train and veil.

The maid of honor usually holds a smaller bouquet and is dressed in formal attire, but according to tradition she should not wear white, black, or red. It is also common to have several bridesmaids and groomsmen.

Best Man

The best man basically has the same tasks as the maid of honor, but he serves the groom. He is the one who organizes the bachelor party. During the wedding, he stands next to the couple, and he is usually responsible for holding the rings during the ceremony. The best man may wear a cravat and waistcoat of a different color than the groomsmen to distinguish himself.

Flower Girl

Flower girls are usually a beloved part of the wedding ceremony and it's not uncommon to have two little flower girls walk down the aisle together. They walk before the bride up to the officiator and spread out flower petals in front of the bride and her father. In earlier times the flower girls symbolized the fruition of life and the couple's future children, but many times today the flower girls are the couple's own children.

The Ring Bearer

The ring bearer is a young boy who traditionally carries the pillow that holds the wedding rings, though these are sometimes fakes for the ceremony so the child doesn't lose them. The ring bearer typically walks down the aisle before the flower girl; however, they will sometimes walk as a pair to give each other confidence. The ring bearer is often a young nephew or a friend's child, but he can also be the couple's own son.

WHO DRESSES THE WEDDING PARTY?

⋙ There are no set rules for who decides what bridesmaids, groomsmen, and flower girls should wear, but typically the one who contributes the most financially has the most say in the matter. If you have very specific ideas or if you want something very extravagant you cannot realistically expect the wedding party to pay for their own attire. Also, remember that it is best for all if each and every person is happy with what they are wearing.

Bridesmaids dressed to match the colors of the wedding.

THE GUESTS:
INVITATIONS TO THE WEDDING

INVITING GUESTS TO a wedding is not easy, and no matter what you do, you probably won't be able to satisfy everyone. Keep in mind that being invited to a wedding is a privilege, not a right. Start by agreeing to only invite those guests who truly want to celebrate with you. If you start with a list of both everyone you *should* invite and those you *want* to invite, the list can become endless.

Determine what your maximum number of guests should be and then both of you should sit down to create a list of people who are important to you. If you are lucky, the number of people you have on your lists are within the maximum capacity you have set. If you end up with more people than your maximum number, you will have to sit down and go over each name one by one.

Family and close friends along with everyone who has invited you to their wedding are the most important guests to invite. If possible, you should try to balance an equal number of guests from the bride's side with a similar number from the groom's side. Another common rule is to always invite your guests' spouses, even if you have not met them in person.

When the guest list is finalized and the invitations are sent out, you should establish an RSVP list where you check off who has responded to the invitation. On this list, you will also mark down any allergies or special food requirements. On page 232 you can find a template to help you keep your guests' responses organized.

Make sure to include any potential restrictions for the wedding on your invitations so your guests know what to expect. If you choose a grandiose affair, you may not want small children attending who can get tired and cry. It's very common to ask guests not to bring children even if some people find this a sensitive subject. As a compromise, you can offer to let children attend during the day but not during the evening. Babies who are nursing, however, are usually allowed even at childfree weddings.

SECURE THE CALENDAR FOR THE WEDDING

≫ When the actual wedding invitations are mailed, the butterflies in your stomach will flutter a little bit. It is considered good etiquette to mail out the invitations three months in advance, and the invitation should state the time, place, dress code, and a request to be notified of any food allergies along with the RSVP date.

THE GUEST LIST

≫ Start preparing the guest list well in advance.

≫ Can't afford to invite everyone? Set a limit.

≫ Do you want to invite everyone? Think about it and talk it through sensibly.

≫ Keep track of your RSVPs. On page 232 you will find a template that will help you do this.

Be specific when describing your intended wedding so your guests can dress accordingly.

THE INVITATION

☞ On page 60 you can read more about how you formulate your invitation as well as what information should be included.

OTHER OCCASIONS WHEN MEN WEAR TUXEDOS

» When playing in a symphonic orchestra

» When working in a fine restaurant, but then with a black bowtie

» When working as a top hat chimney sweep

» When going to prom

» When receiving a doctorate degree

» When a member of a secret society

» When invited to a royal dinner

» When receiving the Nobel Prize

Dress codes—how do your guests know what you mean?

Different dress codes set different tones for the wedding and you should specify on your invitation which dress code is appropriate with the following definitions: formal attire, black tie, or suit and tie. But what do these terms really mean, and what is appropriate for a wedding?

Clarity is essential for your invitation and phrases like "Casual dress code" should be avoided, as they often create stress and confusion among guests. Everyone wants to look nice at a wedding and nobody wants to make a fool out of themselves—therefore you should provide clear instructions for your guests. Make sure that your host and hostess are clear about what you expect so they can help the guests with this.

FORMAL ATTIRE or **"WHITE TIE"** is the most formal of dress codes and not very common for weddings. If the dress code is formal attire, the men can choose between tuxedo and military uniform while the women can choose between long evening gowns and national dress.

The tuxedo consists of a specially cut suit jacket, white tuxedo vest, white tuxedo shirt with a starched chest, and white bowtie with black pants with double stripes along the sides. Vest, waistcoat, and bowtie are always starched white cotton piqué, and if the men want to take it one step further, they can also wear white gloves and a black top hat.

Female guests have a wider range of dress from which to choose. The dress should be long, but sleeves are optional, though the shoulders should be covered in church. The dress can be of any color, but should preferably not be black or white. The dress can be complemented by a beautiful evening bag.

If formal attire is mentioned on the invitation it's important not to show up in a suit, no matter how elegant or expensive it may be. Both groom and guests are best off renting a tuxedo if they do not already have one.

TUXEDO or **"BLACK TIE"** means that the men wear tuxedos with a black or blue jacket. The women can choose to wear a long dress—however, it does not have to be as formal as for the white tie event—or it can even be a shorter evening gown.

A common misconception is that men must wear patent leather shoes with a tuxedo. This is not the case. Loafers are perfectly fine or even regular black leather shoes, but brown shoes or sneakers should be avoided.

The tuxedo is always worn with a black bowtie no matter what color the waistcoat or cummerbund may be. A true gentleman always wears a tuxedo shirt with extra button matching the cufflinks. However, it's best to avoid shirts with tails when wearing a tuxedo. Lately, it has become more common to wear tuxedos at weddings, but they are really meant to be party attire and are not really suitable for church.

SUIT AND TIE is third on the list of formal dress codes and is probably the easiest to understand. A dark suit and tie indicates a formal event where the bride and groom expect all guests to be dressed up for the occasion. The men are expected to wear a dark suit, usually a dark blue one with white shirt, while female guests can choose between a pant suit or a knee length dress of finer quality (long evening gowns should be avoided). The suit is completed with a tie or a colorful bowtie and preferably a pocket square in matching colors. It is also considered proper to wear a watch if the dress code is suit and tie. Shoes should be black.

JACKET is the last official dress code and often makes things a little more complicated. Jacket for men means a suit, but this dress code is more flexible than the formal "dark suit" and it is even acceptable to wear light colored suits.

The women should be dressed more elegantly than everyday wear, but not as grandly as the evening dress expected for suit and tie. Even if it says jacket on the invitation, proper etiquette requires you wear a suit instead of completing the look with jeans.

PROPER DRESS CODE

≫ Do not simply write the word "suit" on your invitation. Rather specify "light colored suit" or "dark suit" to avoid any mishaps in dress code.

FOOT ATTIRE

≫ Always bring one pair of shoes to wear inside and one pair for wearing outside. It's never appropriate to walk around barefoot at a wedding.

MORNING DRESS

≫ The morning coat or cutaway, something between a long coat and a tuxedo, is an unusual item in the United States, but is common in England. It is only worn during the day and is more formal than a suit but less formal than a tuxedo. The jacket for a cutaway should be black and the pants should be gray or gray striped. To follow traditional etiquette, the attire is completed by a gray vest, white shirt, and gray tie or ascot. For less traditional moments, it's common to exchange the gray tie and vest for bright and happy colors. The attire is often worn with a gray or black top hat. This attire is a must at the Royal Ascot race track in England, where the men are accompanied by their ladies dressed in elaborate hats and knee-length dresses in summer colors.

Do you already have everything you can think of? Ask the guests to donate to a charitable organization instead.

THE WEDDING REGISTRY

THE QUESTION OF what you want and what you should ask for as wedding gifts can be a stressful part of the planning. By making a clear list of what you want, you won't have to respond to guests' continuous questions and it will keep you from getting three toasters. It is more fun for both you and your guests if you're happy about the gifts you're receiving! Just remember that the registry is a wish list rather than a list of demands.

An alternative to a wedding registry is to let a department store take care of this for you. The guests will give the store your name and can then see your list. The department store checks off each item on the list as it is purchased for you.

If you don't need or want physical items, you can always wish for experiences. You simply list fun things you would like to do together in the future and let your friends help you actualize your dreams. A third alternative is to wish for contributions to the honeymoon trip. Feel free to send your guests pictures of your honeymoon to show your appreciation.

When Prince William and Kate Middleton got married they asked for charitable contributions, which is a lovely alternative to gifts. The couple made a list of organizations they held dear to their hearts and the guests could choose which to contribute to. Perhaps this is something you would like to do.

When you have completed the gift registry, it is usually the host and hostess who communicate with guests regarding gifts. This is basically something you shouldn't have to deal with, which is usually nice for both the couple and their guests. The person responsible for the gift registry answers the guests' questions about gifts and ensures that there are no duplicates.

> Don't open the gifts during the reception. It takes time and can embarrass the guests. Rather, open them the day after.
>
> Ask someone to keep track of which gift came from what guest. Cards can easily disappear.

Different Kinds of Gifts

THINGS. Most commonly wished for are household items. It is important to be clear here. Tell your guests exactly what you would like. Do you collect glassware? If so, tell your guests what series, brands, and outlets they are from and even which pieces and how many you would like.

EXPERIENCES. Do you have everything you need for the home? Make a list of things you would like to do as newlyweds. Either offer suggestions such as wine tastings or hot air balloon rides or let the guests surprise you. Don't forget to take pictures, write blog entries, or film your experiences so you can share them with those who gave them to you as gifts.

MONEY. If you ask for money, either as a cover charge or as a contribution to the honeymoon, it's easiest to make this request as an addendum to the invitation. Let your guests choose the amount on their own, as a hefty cover charge can be a big turn off for many. You shouldn't look like you're taking advantage of your guests, but many are happy to give generously to your honeymoon rather than buying you a crystal bowl.

CHARITY. Even if you don't want gifts, your guests will most likely want to give you something, and in such cases suggesting a charitable donation is a great alternative. It is also always a nice idea to list your favorite charities for their reference.

Keep in mind that if you ask for a cover charge it is proper etiquette to refrain from asking for any wedding gifts.

Write a Well Thought Out Wish List

STEP 1: THE DISCUSSION

Sit down together and take your time to think about what you actually want and need. Do you need new things for the home or do you want contributions to the honeymoon? Experiences and money are becoming more and more popular to ask for—it just needs to be done tastefully.

STEP 2: FORMULATE THE LIST

The wish list can certainly have a range of items. It is a good idea to have more expensive items for closer friends and family or for people who want to pool together to get you a group gift. Don't forget to also include some budget options for the guests who cannot afford any larger expenses.

STEP 3: ASSIGN A CONTACT PERSON

The key to a successfully planned wedding is to delegate tasks. Assign someone to be in charge of the wish list and let that person handle any and all questions regarding gifts. Usually the host and the hostess handle this task. If you don't have a host and hostess, you can ask your toastmaster or master of ceremonies to take on the wish list.

STEP 4: INFORM YOUR GUESTS

Let your guests know on the invitation that you have a wish list and where your guests can find it. The easiest way is for your contact person to have it or to display it on a wedding website.

STEP 5: OPEN THE GIFTS IN PRIVATE

Are you considering opening the gifts at the reception? Think again! It takes up a lot of time and it's really not fun for the guests to be a part of. It can easily become a competition of who gave the fanciest, most expensive present, and not all guests can spend large amounts of money. Save the opening of the gifts for the day after the wedding; it can be a cozy moment for the two of you. Don't forget to mark down who gives you what.

STEP 6: SAY THANK YOU

Thank you notes are a nice gesture after the wedding. Thank the guest for attending your big day and for the gift you received. If you're ambitious, hand write personal thank you notes to each and every guest.

PRINTED MATERIALS

PRINTED INVITATIONS TO parties have been around for many hundreds of years, and when you mail your wedding invitations you take a very big and exciting step. The wedding is now official! You have notified guests that they are invited, while announcing when and where you are getting married. But you probably have even more information you would like to communicate to your guests, and for that there are several printed items to use. You will probably want your guests to know where they are supposed to sit at the reception and what the menu is. And naturally you will want to be able to thank your guests after the wedding.

CHECKLIST PRINTED MATERIALS

- Save-the-date cards
- Invitations
- Wedding program
- Reception program
- Menu
- Table chart
- Seating map
- Place settings
- Thank you cards

Getting Started

The best way to get started is to get inspired by others, so look around and see what other couples have done for their wedding invitations. Decide if you want pre-printed materials from a vendor or if you plan to create your own. Perhaps you know someone close to you who is creative.

Many arts and crafts stores have ready-made invitations and thank you cards that you can buy or use for inspiration. If you decide to create your own materials, the next step should be to purchase all of the materials you will need to create them. Begin sketching the designs well ahead of time—the closer to the wedding you get, the less time you will have to do it.

Stick to Your Theme

By giving extra time and thought to the various printed items, you will be able to create a uniform design. If you have a theme for the wedding, you can use this as a thread to unify all the printed items and table settings. It is common to have one or several colors as a theme. Include the hue as detailing—for example, in the color of the typography or by tying colored ribbons around all your printed items.

There are many different styles, but the most important thing is that you find your own personal look. Do you want it to be clean and classic or detail oriented and glamorous? If you are worried about overdoing it, the best rule to remember is just to keep it simple.

How Much Will It Cost?

If you decide to order ready-made printed materials, you should contact several vendors and ask for price quotes. Factors such as paper quality, volume, and whether you are mounting the items can affect the price.

But even if you decide to create your own printed items, it can easily get expensive because of high-quality paper, exclusive envelopes, and pricey decorations such as rhinestone-studded clasps. Keep in mind that both invitations and thank you cards are usually mailed. Depending on the weight of the materials, the postage can become substantial. All of this is important to consider when you create your wedding budget.

Things to Keep in Mind

If you want to create your own printed items, you should start by creating one complete set and then go from there. That way, you can figure out how much material you will ultimately need.

If you have found the paper you want, it's best to buy a large enough quantity for all your printed items. You don't want to discover the paper is out of stock when it's time to send out your thank you cards. Also, keep in mind that it will take some time to create all of your items. It could be fun to invite some friends over and make a day of it.

The Most Common Printed Items

INVITATIONS. If you do not send save-the-date cards (see next page), you should send your wedding invitations well in advance to make sure all of your guests can be available on that date.

You should include your names, date, time, and location of your wedding on your invitations, and you should specify dress code and include information regarding the reception after the ceremony. Also ask your guests to notify you of any special food requirements. Include your RSVP deadline along with the contact information for the person who is managing your guest list. Since not everyone will respond on time, it can be a good idea to set a false deadline for RSVPs. It is also a good idea to double-check spelling and addresses, since a misspelled mailing address can cause unnecessary complications.

If there is not enough space on your invitations for all your information, you can always include a loose leaf of paper with the additional information attached. Such information may include practicalities such as directions, transportation options, and lodging suggestions for the guests.

It is perfectly acceptable to want a wedding without any children in attendance. Just make this clear on your invitation by writing in a tasteful manner that you would prefer for everyone to leave the little ones at home.

⋙ Put a little bit of extra time and effort into your invitations. Be playful and personal if you like, but remember to be clear so the guests understand the details.

⋙ Are you planning on using social media to communicate about your wedding? If so, make sure to send out physical invitations as keepsakes for your guests. Nothing beats a beautifully printed invitation!

If you have decided to ask for a cover charge—meaning that you are asking for cash donations to the wedding dinner—you will have to be very clear about this on your invitations. And keep in mind that when you ask for cash donations the proper etiquette is to abstain from any wedding gifts.

If the guests have to pay for their own drinks during the dinner, it should also be mentioned on the invitation. Distinguish also if they will be paying full price for their drinks or if the bar will be at cost, meaning a more nominal sum.

SAVE-THE-DATE CARDS. If you plan to get married abroad or at an unusual (or usual!) time of the year it can be a good idea to send out a save-the-date card so the guests do not make other plans. A save-the-date card is a notification to your guests that they should keep that date open for your wedding. Include your names, the date, and the potential location of the ceremony on the card and inform them that an official invitation will follow shortly. If you want your guests to follow your planning stages up to the wedding, you can also include the link to your wedding home page.

A save-the-date card can be sent out up to nine months before the wedding date. It should include your names, the date, and the potential location of the ceremony. Do something creative with your save-the-date card such as print it on a fridge magnet or a bookmark!

CEREMONY PROGRAM. This is a sheet with information about what will take place during the ceremony and in what order. It is a nice touch, but not a requirement. The ceremony program is handed to guests as they enter the venue.

RECEPTION PROGRAM. This little booklet contains the seating arrangements and the menu. This is a great opportunity to add some fun facts about you as a couple. It is also fun to include trivia about your guests as well. This information is especially appreciated if the guests are not already acquainted and will serve as a great icebreaker at the dinner table.

The reception program is usually placed on each seat, so it is important to have enough for all the guests. If you already have menus at the tables, there is no need to include it in the program.

TABLE CHART. If there are many tables, it is easier for both the servers and the guests if the tables are numbered or given names. The most common custom is to mark the tables with numbers on signs that are placed in the middle of the tables. You can also name your tables after things or places that matter to you.

SEATING CHART. It's a good idea to put up a seating chart at the entrance of the reception hall to help direct your guests to their seats. Mark each table and where each guest will sit.

PLACE SETTINGS. You should make sure that there is a name card at every seat to specify where each guest should sit. The place setting should state the guest's full name, but feel free to be creative when designing these cards!

THANK YOU CARDS. You should send out thank you cards no later than two months after the wedding. On the card, thank your guest for attending your wedding and for their gift. Most couples also include a wedding photo as a keepsake for the guests. The most common thing to do is to send a thank you card to each individual guest who attended your celebration.

Do write personalized handwritten thank you cards if you can. It's always more special to receive a personally written thank you for the gift, such as: "Thank you, Emily, for the amazing painting. We are incredibly happy that you were with us to celebrate our wedding day."

WEDDING THEME

VINTAGE WEDDING, COASTAL SUMMER THEME, or city chic? If your passion is a part of your personality—let it be shown on your wedding day. By choosing a theme and using it to tie together everything from print materials to table settings to the bride's bouquet, you will make the day more personal. Everything will feel cohesive, and the details will bind it all together beautifully.

One simple way to create a theme is to choose one or more colors to use throughout the wedding designs. Think about what color combinations you like and what feelings you want to evoke. Certain combinations are suitable for a glamorous event at a castle, while other colors are better suited for a beach-themed wedding.

Seasonal Colors

Depending on what time of the year you are getting married, some colors are better suited than others. Pastels rarely work during the dark winter months, while fall shades don't seem appropriate during the spring. Here are some tried and true guidelines for each season:

FALL WEDDINGS. Choose a red and orange color scheme similar to the falling leaves or a color in stark contrast to fall colors, like royal blue. There's also an abundance of lovely decorations to be found in nature, such as leaves and pumpkins, to use for ornaments and table settings.

WINTER WEDDINGS. Try using a blue color scheme with white and silver as a complement. Be inspired by ice crystals and frost. Also lanterns, sparklers, and candles will create a lovely atmosphere.

SPRING WEDDINGS. Pastels go well with the bright spring light as well as mint green, pearl white, and gold, which make a great color combination. Let the bright green colors of the spring foliage and flowers set the tone for the decorations both at the ceremony and the reception. Use seasonal flowers in the hair styles and bouquets.

SUMMER WEDDINGS. Summer is the favorite time to get married, because nature is bursting with happy colors. Bring summer into the ceremony venue, decorate the reception hall, and use seasonal flowers when decorating the tables. Colors such as fuchsia and lilac are beautiful for a summer wedding. However, bear in mind that summer flowers do not last very long before they start to wilt. Ask your florist for suggestions.

Matching

Print materials and flowers can definitely have the same color scheme. Even napkins and napkin rings can be nice to match, but don't overdo it. Having pink chair slips, pink tablecloths, pink napkins, pink flowers, and pink dresses can seem a little bit over the top.

Rather, choose two strong colors that complement each other—for example, green and fuchsia. Then complement them with a neutral color, such as ivory. If you want more colors, they should be in the same color range. Red, orange, and rusty brown are nice. That way you can have one main color and use the other hues as detailing.

If you intend to wear a dress, vest, or necktie in a certain color, you should first be sure that it suits you. Yellow, orange, and blue can be difficult colors, and spending weeks looking for silk ribbons in a certain hue can stress anyone out. Choose a common color or start researching early on to find the right color for you.

CHOOSE A COLOR SCHEME
Here are a few color combinations that go well together.

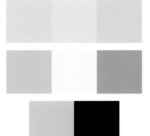

ROMANTIC
Light pink, vanilla, and light apricot
Light green apple, ivory, and gold
Dusty rose and black

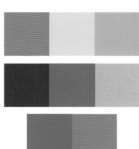

BRILLIANT COLORS
Fuchsia, light pink, and orange
Plum, dark green, light gray or silver
Dark green and fuchsia

ALLURING
Orange, brown, and corn blue
Light yellow and fuchsia
Mint green and brown

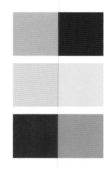

CLASSIC
Silver and dark blue
Sand and light blue
Burgundy and gold

Anna & Peter
22 august

TRANSPORTATION

IT IS EASY TO forget the necessary step of planning how you will travel between the ceremony venue and the reception hall. It's important to think about where the ceremony venue is located in relation to the reception hall. Remember, it could rain and you certainly wouldn't want to walk through the mud in your wedding clothes or have to dash to the reception hall through a downpour. The trip offers a moment for you to be alone as a newly wedded couple. It also gives you a chance to make a grand entrance when you arrive at the reception hall.

Also, think about logistics for your guests if the ceremony venue is far away from the reception hall. Your wedding guests will also need transportation, and if you are not going to rent a bus for them you will have to coordinate properly. Let your host and hostess take care of this part well ahead of time.

THINK ABOUT:

⟫ How far you will have to travel

⟫ How many guests need transportation

⟫ Transportation budget

⟫ What kind of people you are and what suits you best

ADVENTUROUS HELICOPTER RIDE

Why not take a helicopter ride after the wedding ceremony? Take the opportunity to enjoy this moment together and make a memorable entrance at the reception hall.

Pros: Is not just transportation but an experience.

Cons: Your hairdo might fall apart and the ride requires a larger budget and some additional time.

CLASSIC CAR

The most common is to travel by car. But perhaps you can swap your usual Volvo for something a little more festive? A glamorous limousine, a fast sports car, or a beautiful classic automobile—think about which car suits you best and what complements the theme. Perhaps you know someone who can lend you a nice car for the wedding?

Pros: A wide range of offerings.

Cons: Not very original. Can get expensive.

> ⋙ Think outside the box—perhaps you prefer transportation such as a kayak, scooter, or skateboard!

A PEACEFUL BOAT RIDE

If you get married close to the water, you can always choose a boat for transportation. If you rent a larger model, you can even do the wedding toast with your guests there. Rowing in a skiff might look great in pictures but for that you need calm seas and a short distance to go.

Pros: Relaxed and peaceful.
Cons: Not ideal for people who get seasick.

ROMANTIC HORSE AND BUGGY

Horse and buggy is a classic mode of wedding transportation and has been used by royals and "regular" couples throughout the centuries. The romantic country atmosphere is perfect if your wedding takes place outside the city limits, and the most simple of buggies can be decorated with flowers and become remarkable.

Pros: Romantic!
Cons: An open carriage is not the best if it starts to rain. Moves slowly.

ECO-FRIENDLY BIKING

If you want to be eco-friendly and enjoy your surroundings at the same time—ride bikes. Choose between individual bikes, a tandem bike, or one with a carriage.

Pros: Cheap, easy, and can give you a lot of fun wedding pictures. Easy to move around if you wed in the city.
Cons: Can get difficult for the person peddling. High risk of getting your clothes dirty.

FLOWERS

EVERYONE LOVES FLOWERS. They can enhance everything from the bride's appearance to the atmosphere in the reception hall. Establish your flower budget from the beginning to make sure you don't let the expenses get out of hand. It is standard practice to use five to ten percent of the total budget for the flowers.

Wedding flowers do not necessarily have to be massive arrangements. It is just as beautiful to place single stems in vases. Use seasonal flowers to keep within budget and let your imagination run wild with the endless possibilities. Decorate the tables with candles, candy bowls, and ribbons to complete the floral decorations.

Even bridesmaid bouquets can take a toll on your flower budget. Why not give your bridesmaids a single beautiful flower to hold in their hands? Lilies and daisies are most beautiful when they stand alone.

It is always a good idea to speak to both your florist and your dress store about the bridal bouquet; certain dress styles are best matched with certain types of flowers. Flowers can be used to enhance or hide aspects of the bride's body, depending on her body type (read more about choosing the wedding bouquet based on body shape on page 116).

What do you do if you like the idea of tossing your bouquet but you don't want to literally throw away your costly flowers? The solution is called the "toss bouquet." Ask your florist to create a simplified version of your bouquet for you to toss to your friends.

>> Remember to ask about any possible allergies your guests may have on your wedding invitation—not just food allergies, but also pollen allergies.

Have your bridesmaids' smaller bouquets match your wedding bouquet in both color and style for a unified look.

The Most Common Flower Arrangements

Flowers are for more than just the bridal bouquet. Try to keep the same style for the bridal bouquet, bridesmaid bouquets, boutonnière, and decorations—the flowers will have the most visual impact that way.

BRIDAL BOUQUET. There are many shapes and styles to choose from. One tip is to consider both body shape and dress style when choosing your bridal bouquet (read more about this on page 116). Many brides also match their bouquets with the wedding colors, but that is certainly not a requirement.

BOUTONNIÈRE. The groom usually carries a flower on the left lapel of his suit jacket, and some groomsmen choose to do so as well. For a unified look, it is a nice touch to use the same kind of flower as one used in the bridal bouquet.

BRIDESMAID BOUQUET. Many bridesmaids carry a smaller version of the bridal bouquet for the ceremony. It can also be used as the toss bouquet if the bride doesn't want to throw away her own.

HAIR DECORATIONS. It is popular to enhance the bridal hairstyle with a flower. Check with your florist ahead of time to be sure the flower won't wilt before the day is over.

WEDDING FLOWERS. Check carefully with the ceremony venue for what is offered and what is allowed. If you're getting married outside, there is a greater possibility of decorating without limitations than at an indoor wedding.

CONFETTI PETALS. A beautiful alternative to tossing rice or blowing soap bubbles at the married couple after the ceremony is to throw flower petals. However, fresh flower petals do tend to leave spots on the dresses and may wilt ahead of time. There are synthetic flower petals you can buy, but remember that they will have to be cleaned up after they have been thrown.

PARTY DECORATIONS. Depending on what color and what sort of flowers you choose, you can set whatever atmosphere you want with these flowers. Table settings are usually the most important arrangements, but it's always nice to have a few other arrangements around the room.

CAKE. Flowers are the hottest trend in cake decorations right now. Choose between real or sugar flowers. Remember not to place real flowers on pieces that will be eaten; instead, have a shield between cake and flowers.

A corsage for the bridesmaids enhances the bridal bouquet! Also feel free to decorate the church with flowers. Tossing flower petals can be used as a great alternative to rice.

These flowers are some of the most common.
From left to right: Calla lily, orchid, red rose, lily of the
valley, lilac, ranunculus, spray rose, columbine, gerbera
daisy, hydrangea, ivory rose, and peony.

The most common flowers, all in one bouquet.

Seasonal Flowers

If you absolutely have to have your horse-drawn carriage decorated with fall foliage while you hold a bouquet of summer blooms, there will definitely be some challenges.

Choosing out of season flowers can make your flower budget skyrocket, so be sure to research early on whether the flowers you want will be in season for your wedding.

Perhaps you're willing to compromise, and if so, find a skilled florist who can offer less expensive substitutes for what you were thinking of. Give the florist an idea of your picture perfect wedding with details such as clothing and reception theme. Then, give the florist free rein to create an appropriate arrangement with seasonal flowers. That way you will get more for your money than if you have exacting specifications.

If you want to dry your bouquet and save it as a keepsake, spray it with hairspray so it does not collect as much dust.

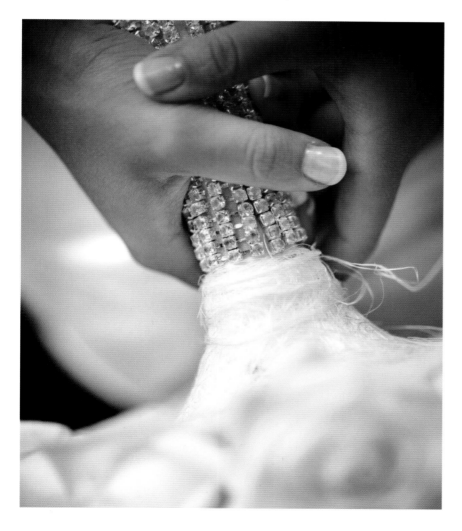

Decorate the stem of the bouquet with beads or pearls, or wrap it in a beautiful casing such as the one shown here.

Spring Flowers

TULIPS. Beautiful in both the bridal bouquet and in table arrangements. Stick to one color for the bouquet and just add some green as an accent.

LILIES OF THE VALLEY. Luxurious, especially with camellias and gardenias. Especially popular after Kate Middleton had them in her bouquet.

FREESIAS. Beautiful with roses. Look great as hair decorations.

RANUNCULUS. A perfect match with peonies. Great for table decorations.

PEONIES. Very popular in bridal bouquets. By placing one peony in a glass bowl filled with water, you will have a perfect table decoration.

MAGNOLIAS. Majestic together with a bare branch and a lot of winding leaves. However, this flower is quite expensive, so if you plan to decorate a lot of tables, you may want to place one stem in water accompanied by roses.

LILACS. Only bloom for a few weeks during spring, but create a lovely, relaxed atmosphere. Opt for flowers on the branch since they have a tendency to wilt fairly quickly off the branch. Also keep in mind that many people are allergic to lilacs.

Summer Flowers

SUNFLOWERS. A single sunflower looks wonderful in the bouquet. At the reception, a great look is the flower floating on a zinc plate filled with water.

LAVENDER. Nice to have in pots on the tables, or adorn with a ribbon and place them on the table. Can also be nice to give to guests as a keepsake beside their plate.

CARNATIONS. Tie carnations of many colors into a tight bouquet for a lasting impression. It looks like a carpet of colors. Also does well in buttonholes.

ROSES. Long lasting and gorgeous. Looks delightful when several large-leaved roses are combined into one large rose. In season throughout the year.

SWEET PEAS. Create the bouquet in shades of purple and pink. Beautiful when using the vines to place the blooms on top of a bouquet of roses. Are also perfectly suited for large arrangements in the middle of the table.

A spring bouquet of peonies and roses.

A light spring bouquet of lilacs.

White bouquets are suitable for every season.

A summer bouquet of pink carnations.

Fall Flowers

CHRYSANTHEMUM. Is beautiful as one single stem together with green leaves in the bridal bouquet.

GERBERA DAISIES. Mix several colors in the bouquet. Perfect for hair decorations.

FALL HYDRANGEA. Great for wreaths and garlands. Works well as table decorations or as decorations on pedestals.

ORCHIDS. Elegant as a single stem tied to a steel frame. Gives a clean impression. Also nice with a base of rununculus and just one or two orchids at the top of the bouquet.

GLADIOLUS. Beautiful when placed in tall vases on the floor or in windows. Works well as a bouquet for simple dresses.

DAHLIAS. Garden flowers that bloom during late summer into early fall. Come in many shapes, heights, and colors. Use them as fall arrangements along with squash and pumpkins on the tables.

Gerbera daisies in fall orange colors.

Robust colors do well in winter.

Winter Flowers

SNOWDROPS. Use together with pinecones for small table arrangements. Adorable in bouquets with a base of white lilies tied together into a round ball. Needs support to keep from drooping.

HYACINTH. At its most beautiful when in half-bloom and is best suited for use in small pots at the middle of the tables.

CAMELLIAS. Ideal both alone in a wild bunch and together with roses and freesias.

NERINE. Lovely at the middle of a bouquet filled with bright pink roses or tied around the bouquet. Are also suitable for a long-stemmed bouquet.

AMARYLLIS. Are only needed sparingly. They can easily be cut down and placed in glass bowls as table decorations. They are also lovely when tied upside down in windows.

TULIPS. A bouquet of tulips is truly an elegant bridal bouquet. There are many varieties to choose from, including some more unusual and luxurious ones.

Pastel colors are best in spring.

Elegant winter bouquet of white tulips and roses.

IMMORTALIZE YOUR WEDDING

YOU'LL ALMOST CERTAINLY FLIP through your wedding photos every once in a while for the rest of your lives, and because of this it's worth the money to hire a professional photographer. Many couples let a close friend or relative take the photos, and perhaps they will manage to get a couple of great shots of you, but do you really want to rely on luck for your wedding day?

If you decide to hire a professional photographer, there are many who specialize in wedding photography. But in order to find the right photographer, you will need to book well in advance.

Wedding photography can be had in various price ranges, but generally you will get what you pay for. If you're concerned about the cost, perhaps you can hire a better photographer for only an hour rather than hiring a less expensive one for the whole day. The quantity does not matter as much as the quality. During the evening you can let your guests take the pictures. Guests usually enjoy being given disposable cameras during the wedding so they can take part in the photography.

Choose the Right Photography Style

Classic portrait, event, or fashion photography? There are so many styles to choose from, but not all photographers can do all kinds of photography. No matter if you want traditional portraits or event pictures all day long, you should choose your photographer with care.

The most common practice is to hire a photographer for classic portraits. Shooting the portaits takes place in a studio or outdoors, and the image is arranged and the couple is eternalized forever in classic poses. Sometimes they will take photos of the couple with the maid of honor, best man, close family, and even a group photo of all the guests.

Another alternative is to choose an event photographer and let him or her follow you and your guests throughout the day. The photographer eternalizes the day as it happened, without styling the photographs too much. Spontaneity and snapshots are keywords here. Event photography is becoming more and more advanced, and some photographers even edit their shots afterward to create a retro feeling, for example, to evoke the style of an earlier era.

Don't forget to ask someone to film the ceremony and reception!

A third alternative, which has become very popular lately, is to hire a lifestyle photographer. The style is inspired by fashion photography, and the photographer arranges the photos at various locations, usually outdoors, and includes portrait photography.

Choose the Right Photographer

It's a good idea to meet photographers to make sure the chemistry is right between you, since it is important that you feel comfortable in front of their camera. If you are met with courtesy and professionalism from the start, it is very likely you will have a good working relationship. On the other hand, if you find a photographer who doesn't take your calls and haggles with you on the fee and contract, it's probably safest to look for someone else. The last thing you need is to have problems with your photographer on your wedding day. Trust your instincts and ask for references or ask friends if they can recommend someone. Besides trusting your gut, there are other rules of thumb to follow:

≫ Always choose a professional photographer. You most likely know someone with professional equipment and this person might manage to get a few nice pictures for you, but that is a far cry from a professional photographer who has both the technical skills and experience it takes to guarantee that you will get your dream photos.

≫ Always book well in advance. Good photographers are booked early, so if you can, book close to a year ahead of time.

PHOTOS YOU CAN'T MISS!

≫ Spontaneous snapshots
≫ Traditional portraits
≫ The rings
≫ The bride's bouquet
≫ The dress
≫ Bride with bridesmaids
≫ Groom with groomsmen
≫ The couple with family
≫ The couple with all guests
≫ The hair style
≫ The kiss

≫ Don't get stuck on just one background or a certain style of photos; instead, think about what kind of styles work for you. Are you a couple that loves to read? If so, perhaps some photos in a library would be nice.

A best friend with a good quality camera is not equal to a professional photographer. Think about this carefully. You only have one chance to get it right.

Draw up a contract with the photographer and review it thoroughly. It should clearly state what is included in the price, the exact cost, and when payments are due, as well as the delivery date for the photographs. There are no standard contracts for photographers, so you will have to negotiate your own. Usually the photographer has an assortment of packages to choose from.

Check what is included in the price. If you are only getting low-resolution images, you won't be able to make enlargements afterward. Certain photographers offer a large number of photographs, but without any editing included, while others offer a smaller number of photographs that have been edited in detail. Sometimes they include an album or a photo book or perhaps a set of developed pictures.

If you're planning to take photos outside, you should have a backup plan in case of bad weather. It's a good idea to have a place inside where you can take your photos, or keep an umbrella and rain boots handy. Other things that might come in handy during the photo shoot are powder for shiny faces, water, combs, band-aids for blisters, sugary candy for low blood sugar, and lip gloss.

CREATE MEMORIES

Make enlargements. Choose the best photo and turn it into a piece of art. A beautiful canvas painting or a really grand photograph makes for a perfect living room piece.

Create a photo book. Having a difficult time choosing just one picture? Create a whole book with your favorite wedding memories. Many photographers offer exclusively bound photo books for an extra fee.

Frame it. The most classic and common way to commemorate your day is to frame your wedding photo.

Thank your guests. Don't forget to send a card to your wedding guests to thank them for making your day memorable.

Classic album. Do you prefer to create things on your own and to write your own comments with a beautiful pen? If so, the classic photo album is the way to commemorate your wedding day.

HONEYMOON

MANY COUPLES CHOOSE to leave for the honeymoon right after the wedding, but expenses and time-consuming planning for the wedding can often lead to a postponement of the honeymoon. To make sure the honeymoon actually takes place, you should include its expenses in the wedding budget. Sit down together and talk about your dream and what is realistic. If you dream about palm trees, white sand beaches, clear turquoise waters, and lazy days in the sun, it can end up costing you a lot, as this is a dream many share. For example, many couples travel to Tahiti for their honeymoon and therefore it has become a very expensive destination. Make sure you agree on your destination and how much you want to spend. It can be a good idea to open up an account where your guests have the option of contributng to your honeymoon as a wedding gift.

Set a date for when you want to leave, even if you haven't booked your tickets.

> Don't have enough time and money available? Choose a weekend trip to a big city instead.

TIPS FOR A MEMORABLE HONEYMOON

Choose your hotel with care. Find a hotel that will cater to your needs. If you're traveling alone, it's always nice to stay at a quiet hotel where you can enjoy your privacy without any babies crying in the hallways or obnoxious partiers at the poolside. Many travel agents offer special hotels that are best suited for honeymooners.

King-size beds—not double beds. Be specific when you book your room so you get a big bed instead of two smaller ones pushed together. The honeymoon is supposed to be a time of closeness and intimacy and the bed is always more inviting when there aren't any gaps in the middle.

Ask for attention. When booking and checking in don't be shy about letting people know you're there on your honeymoon. Airlines, hotels, and restaurants often offer upgrades or something extra to honeymooners.

Take advantage of carry on luggage. Standing around waiting for your luggage at baggage claim isn't fun. Be sure to pack a change of clothing in your carry on in case something goes wrong.

Seasonal Travel Destinations

If you have a preferred travel destination, check to see when it is the best season to travel there—ending up in the middle of the rainy season is not a fun experience. If you want to leave right after the wedding, you may have to compromise when it comes to choice of travel destination.

AFRICA. Perhaps South Africa sounds like a good idea with safari, wine, and golf? November to April is the best time to go weather-wise, but if you want to go on a safari, the best time can vary greatly depending on country and what animals roam there.

ASIA. Asia with Thailand at the tip is a popular destination for the Scandinavians. The rainy season begins in June and lasts until October, but rain showers can also occur in November. May and June on the other hand are very hot and humid.

ITALY. A honeymoon in Tuscany is best during spring and fall—avoid the middle of the summer when it's too dry, hot, and crowded. The classic honeymoon destinations of Lugaon, Cuomo, and Garda lakes in northern Italy are also magical around this time of year.

CARIBBEAN CRUISE. Do you dream of a cruise around the Caribbean islands? If so, it's important to remember that hurricane season lasts from July to October. It's safe to travel there in November, or you can choose one of the islands south of the hurricane belt—Trinidad, Tobago, Aruba, Curaçao, and Bonaire—at any time. Most cruises leave from the US, and it can be worth buying a travel package where airfare is included.

THE MALDIVES. The Maldives are best visited from December to April. After that comes the rainy season, which lasts until November. The Seychelles is a great travel destination year round, but best between May and September. Just remember that the winds are from southeast or northwest half of the year. If you want clear waters during your stay, you would do best to stay on the northwest of the islands if you visit between May and September.

MEDITERRANEAN CRUISE. Cruising around the Mediterranean is best done in May, June, September, and October. Avoid July and August when there are just too many people and it gets too hot.

NORTHERN SCANDINAVIA. Are you considering an active vacation in the northern parts of Scandinavia with its dramatic mountains and lakes? If so, bear in mind that the midnight sun can only been seen north of the Arctic Circle and during the period from June to the middle of July if you are far north, otherwise only during June. During July, the mosquitoes are relentless, but they taper off in August.

THE RIVIERA. The Mediterranean Riviera is most expensive to visit during July and August when it is at its warmest and has the most visitors. Great deals can be found for June and September.

SOUTH PACIFIC AND AUSTRALIA. Dreaming of a luxurious bungalow over turquoise waters in the South Pacific? Remember that such a trip is both expensive and complicated—those destinations are actually in the middle of the ocean on the other side of the world! In these cases, it's best to book a package deal. The best times for the South Pacific are March until October and, as we all know, Australia has summer when we have winter. The best combination is to first visit Australia and New Zealand and then take a trip to Fiji, Tonga, Tahiti, or any of the other islands in the vicinity.

USA. New York is best in May, September, and October. Avoid the summer when it's too hot and too many tourists visit. Cruising in a convertible up the California coastline is best during August and September, as you can experience the harvest time of the local vineyards. Florida is best in January until April when there is no rainy season, hurricanes, and hot ocean temperatures as in the summer. In May the humidity rises and it gets really hot after the hurricanes arrive.

HONEYMOON

⫸ The word "honeymoon" is in most languages called "honey-month." This is in reference to the first month after the wedding, which is known as the sweetest and most tender month. It's the month when the couple really gets to know each other and the everyday chores have not yet taken over. But the term also indicates the mead that was given to the bride and groom in the olden days, and was served during the wedding and the month thereafter. People have been drinking mead since the dawn of time, and it consists of water and honey fermented into an alcoholic beverage. Mead is no longer served but the name "honeymoon" has remained. In Anglo-Saxon countries, it's traditional to take the honeymoon right after the wedding day, which we often see in movies when the couple takes off right after the reception.

THE BRIDE

A Dream in Tulle or Sixties Chic?

Let's be honest, you've probably dreamed about your wedding day since you were a child, imagining yourself standing there in a long white gown, saying "I do" to your soul mate. Even if you no longer want a meringue-style dress, you do want to look your very best and be happy with your appearance on your special day. The wedding day is a day you will remember for the rest of your life and is one of the rare moments when all eyes will be on you.

There are many pieces that will need to fall into place for you to feel at your very best. Everything from hair to gown to shoes are pieces that make up the complete look, and there are a few things to consider when choosing what to wear, no matter if you want a princess dress or a short 1960s-style dress.

THE WEDDING DRESS

DESPITE THE FACT THAT THE WEDDING DRESS is an obvious part of most weddings, it is actually a fairly recent tradition. Even though it has always been important to dress up for weddings, in the olden days, not everyone was able to afford a new gown for the occasion. Instead, many people put on their best church clothing or borrowed something from a close friend or relative. Most people could only afford to own one nice dress, and for practical reasons, this was always black; since black could be worn for funerals, it was the most sensible color to have. In Scandinavia in particular, many people married in black for this reason.

A splendid wedding dress was a luxury dating back to the French royal court and was reserved for the wealthy elite. These dresses were the height of fashion and made with rich materials—the more material and the more expensive they were indicated the family's status. The white wedding dress was made popular in the 1800s by Queen Victoria of England; after she wore white to her wedding to Prince Albert, it became popular among the well-to-do.

In the 1900s, fashion began to dictate the style of wedding dresses. Materials became less expensive, culture and religion no longer had the same impact, and people married out of love rather than tradition and the need to make advantageous connections. Dresses became shorter, tighter, and longer depending on which decade and what trend was in vogue.

Today, it is a given that the bride will choose whatever she is comfortable in and what fits her personality. Do you want to get married in jeans? Go ahead, but remember to let your guests know in advance so they can follow suit.

Most brides choose to buy a dress for their wedding, but if you don't want to get married in a traditional gown, you should think about what other occasions you can use the dress for later. You can always alter the dress—perhaps adding some straps or detailing in another color? If you want to save money, you can even rent a wedding gown or buy one secondhand.

There is a wedding dress for every body type. Try different styles to see what kind of dress enhances your body and personality best.

FIND YOUR STYLE!

Create a mood board from magazine clippings and pictures of dresses you like. It helps put things in perspective and certain details will stand out to you, making it easier to identify the style that works best for you.

Many brides choose a long, white dress in a fancy material, but a wedding gown does not have to be white. It is compleletly acceptable to choose another color.

Do you want to look romantic, glamorous, or trendy? Choose the style you want and then follow your own criteria for choosing the dress and accessories.

Various cuts for the wedding dress

There's no longer just one wedding dress style that's in fashion. There are many different cuts and lengths in the stores, and the style of the dress sets the tone for both the wedding and your overall look. Base your dress selection first and foremost on your personal taste and style.

A-LINE. It is said that this classy but feminine model was designed by the house of Dior with inspiration from the Eiffel Tower. The shape is just like the name suggests—outlined like a capital A. It's narrow at the shoulders and gets wider evenly as the skirt reaches the floor.

MERMAID. It is not that difficult to see why this dress is reminiscent of the mermaid in the fairytale. The dress is tight all the way down to the thighs or the knees where it dramatically flares out like a fishtail.

BALLGOWN. A model inspired by fairytale princesses like Cinderella. The dress has a classic, tight-hugging bodice and a voluminous skirt, usually in tulle.

TEA-LENGTH. This model has its origins in the calf-length dresses that used to be worn during tea parties in the olden days.

KNEE-LENGTH. The knee-length dress that pays homage to the sixties and Jackie Onassis has recently come back in fashion. This dress is common at weddings where the bride doesn't want to be dressed too formally and where the dress code is suit and tie.

ASYMMETRICAL. In recent years, the wedding world has been taken over by dresses with various asymmetrical cuts, which offer an exciting and playful dynamic. For example, an asymmetrical dress can have a skirt that's longer in the back than in the front, or it can be a one-shoulder piece.

EMPIRE WAIST. This dress evokes the Greek goddesses of myth. The bust is defined, but beyond that the dress flows freely. The dress is often in chiffon, since that material is light and flowy.

BOLERO. A bolero is a short, fitted jacket, which is perfect to wear over a strapless dress.

TRAIN. A dress with a train is best suited for the grandiose wedding. The train can be anything from six inches to longer than six and a half feet in length.

A-LINE

MERMAID

BALLGOWN

TEA LENGTH

KNEE LENGTH

ASYMMETRICAL

ASYMMETRICAL

EMPIRE WAIST

BOLERO

TRAIN

Dress Based on Body Shape

There are certain guidelines that are worth following in order to find the dress that perfectly flatters your figure.

APPLE SHAPE. If you have a classic apple shape, you have small shoulders, a small chest, and your weight is focused around the torso. You look especially great in a classic empire waist dress, which is defined under the bust with the rest of the gown free flowing. Tight-fitting dresses probably do not flatter your figure as much, since they make your body look more square than curvy.

PEAR SHAPE. A small chest and waist in combination with larger thighs and bottom is a classic pear shape. Draw attention to your small chest with a tight bodice and a wide skirt that hides your thighs. Be inspired by the classic fifties shape and style icon Grace Kelly and find a dress with a little bit of tulle under the skirt.

HOURGLASS SHAPE. Just as the name indicates, you have a small and clearly defined waist. Your shoulders and hips are proportional and are wider than the waist and you probably have a larger chest. Accentuate your curves with a dress that is tight at the waist, such as the mermaid dress. You're physique is also well suited for larger skirts as long as the dress has a defined shape.

TUBE SHAPE. The tube body shape has broad shoulders and a wide waist. Your hips are fairly narrow and you have a flat behind, while your thighs are thick. The most flattering dress for you is the A-line, preferably with a low-cut neckline right where the dress flares out under the bust. Try to avoid tight-fitting dresses.

> ⇛ If you are tall, accentuate your height with long lines and material that falls flatteringly on your body. Accentuate your waist, not your hips!
>
> ⇛ Are you short and petite? Accentuate your feminine look with lace and tulle.

A plunging back makes a tight dress sensual and feminine.

Lacing or Zipper?

If you're planning on selling your gown after the wedding, you should keep in mind that secondhand dresses go for a lot less than the original price.

Most dresses are closed with either a zipper or by lacing in the back. If you tend to fluctuate in weight, you're better off choosing a dress that laces closed. With lacing, you don't have to worry about not fitting into the dress in case you happen to gain a few pounds before the wedding. A dress with a zipper, however, runs the risk of being too big if you lose weight or too small if you gain weight. Just bear in mind that a dress with lacing is nearly impossible to put on by yourself. It also takes some practice for the person who closes the dress for you to get a really pretty result. If you buy a vintage or secondhand dress, it's always easier to find a lace-up dress that will fit you; the lacing is more forgiving and you can even choose a dress either a size smaller or larger without worrying if it will fit or not.

A dress with a zipper will usually have to be altered. You do have the benefit of being able to dress yourself though. This can be practical if you're shy or prefer to ready yourself on your own.

Do you like the look of a row of small buttons down your back? Closing each and every button—and then having your partner unbutton them that night—can be quite frustrating. It's better to choose a dress that has decorative buttons down the back and a hidden zipper. That way you can have the look, but you can get in and out of the dress easily.

The most important thing, however, is that you love your dress. How much fun would a practical dress be if you had your heart set on a different design? Think practically, but follow your heart!

A dress with a long row of buttons in the back is beautiful, but it requires patience. Avoid frustration by choosing a dress with decorative buttons and a hidden zipper!

How to Find the Prettiest Wedding Dress

You should feel at your most beautiful on your wedding day and the dress plays a big part in this. Start by choosing a dress that fits you perfectly, and then create a complete look around it. To make sure you will be completely satisfied, it is important to be systematic.

- Start looking early. You should begin at least six months before the wedding. There is a big chance you will have to order your dress, and it is always wise to leave enough time for alterations.

- Keep your budget in mind. Wedding dresses are available in all price ranges, and it is good to set your price ceiling before you fall in love with a dress you cannot afford. If you know how much you can spend on the dress, it is easier for the consultant to help you.

- Find the style that suits you best. Think about what style of dress you love. Make a list of what is most important to you and then create a mood board with magazine clippings and pictures from the Internet.

- Let the search be an experience. Allow plenty of time for trying on dresses and bring your friends, bridesmaids, family—anyone who will enjoy the experience with you. Don't forget to schedule a nice lunch in between to replenish your energy before you continue your search.

- Try them on! Take advantage of the store consultant's expertise, and don't hesitate to try on styles that you might not have considered before. Trust your instinct because you will know when you find the right dress.

- Try on your dress close to the wedding. Don't forget to try on your dress to make sure it still fits perfectly. Whether you like it or not, it's not unusual to gain or lose weight during the wedding preparations.

KEEP IN YOUR BAG WHEN TRYING ON WEDDING DRESSES

- Pen and paper to write down your favorite styles, prices, and the stores in which you found them.

- A camera to take pictures so you can remember what they look like. Just make sure to ask the staff for permission to photograph their designs.

- A bottle of water and a snack to keep your energy up.

- The right kind of undergarments can be the deciding factor in how well the dress looks on you!

A long train can be impressive, but it does require that someone helps you to keep it in shape when dressing and during the ceremony.

Wedding Dress ER

A white dress in an expensive fabric can be beautiful but can also cause problems. Here are some tips for avoiding emergencies on your big day.

STAINS. Outdoor photography, red wine, and dancing on a dirty floor! When the wedding day is over, your dress will probably not be as white as it was before, but to get a stain on the dress before the wedding is dreadful. A dress that is sensitive to water needs a well thought out plan to resolve the problem.

- Wet baby wipes can remove most stains.

- Pollen stains from the wedding bouquet are tempting to brush off, but you risk rubbing them into the dress. Use the sticky side of a piece of tape to carefully remove the powder.

- If the stain does not come away, you can hide the damage with some white chalk.

- White wine is a great solution for removing red wine stains. Just be careful on sensitive materials.

- If nothing else works, you will have to camouflage the stain. A broach, bow, or shawl can help!

TEARING. One misplaced step on the train and a tear is unavoidable. Unfortunately, there are no miracles to resolve this except some adjustments.

- Needle and thread will make sure that the dress stays intact well enough.

- Tape up the dress with a clear, heavy tape on the inside of the dress.

- If the tear is placed in a convenient enough place, it can be covered by a bow, broach, or shawl.

WRINKLES. It's important to hang the dress up before you wear it so it stays free of wrinkles. These can appear at a moment's notice and are difficult to get rid of. Certain dresses can be ironed, but those come few and far between. Many times you'll need a professional steamer to get rid of wrinkles. If you only have a tiny wrinkle, you might be able to get rid of it by holding a steam iron about three inches from the dress. Never use water and especially not water from a steam iron. It can stain the dress.

SIZE. This miscalculation is best avoided by trying on the dress a week before the wedding so there is enough time to alter it if necessary. If the dress does not fit on the wedding day, you will have to make do. If the dress is too big, you can pad the bust. Safety pins on the inside of the dress can help adjust it somewhat. If the dress is too small, you'll have to open up the zipper a little and cover the shoulders with a shawl. Try to stand in such a way that it isn't noticeable during the photo shoot and change into a party dress for the evening.

It is so easy to tear the train! Don't forget to carry a needle and thread in your purse to resolve any mishaps.

Caring for Your Wedding Dress

⫸ Keep in mind that different materials need to be treated in different ways. Ask the staff at the dress shop how to care for your dress in the best way possible. Certain materials wrinkle easier than others; this is important to keep in mind if you're planning on transporting your dress.

As vintage styles are back in fashion, many brides have started looking into family attics to find dresses. Perhaps you want to pass your own dress on to your daughter or maybe you want to save it as a keepsake. Wedding gowns are often fragile, but if you take proper care of it, the dress can last for a lifetime.

TRANSPORTATION. If you are planning to travel with your dress, you should keep it in a garment bag that is water resistant, preferably with a handle for a better grip. It's also a plus if you can fold the garment bag, as it will be easier to carry and store. If you are taking your dress on a flight, you should contact the airline to make sure they offer a place for it on board. Sometimes the cabin crew will offer a space for your dress behind one of their own seats. If this isn't possible and you have to pack it in your suitcase, make sure to seal the dress in plastic to ensure it won't come in contact with moisture.

CLEANING AND CARE. Use a reputable dry cleaner if you need to clean or wash your dress. Many materials cannot handle moisture or heat, so make sure to ask for cleaning and care directions at the store when you purchase it. Most gowns will include laundry care labels. If something goes wrong even though you've followed the washing instructions, you should file a complaint. A leaky steam iron can easily stain silk, and certain other materials that might have plastic in them will melt at high heat. The best thing to do is to steam iron the dress to get rid of any wrinkles and creases.

STORAGE. Keep the dress stored in a fabric closet or an acid free, unbuffered cardboard box to prevent yellowing and mold. Feel free to ask the staff at the dress shop if they sell specific storage boxes for wedding dresses. If you want your dress to be passed down to your children, it is especially important to store it properly.

A dress that is packed for transport will easily get wrinkled—allow the dress enough time to hang for the wrinkles to come undone.

THE BRIDAL BOUQUET

⋙ Making your own bouquet might not sound difficult, but choosing the right flowers and arranging them does require some know-how. Think twice about making your own bouquet before you decide to do so, because you run the risk of it falling apart before you say "I do."

THE BRIDAL BOUQUET IS NOT MEANT TO HIDE you from prying eyes; it is there to enhance you as a bride. Let the bouquet help accentuate your figure, but be careful not to let the flowers overshadow you.

It is important for the dress, hair, and flowers to be in harmony. In general, the bouquet should have a similar shape as your body. A small bride requires a small bouquet and a tall bride should have something with long stems, while the curvaceous bride can afford a more sprawling bouquet. One great way to check this is that you should be able to hold the bouquet directly in front of you without anyone behind you being able to see it.

These days, it's trendy to have a color scheme where details are matched to create a unified look. Even when it comes to the choice of flowers for the bridal bouquet, it's elegant to incorporate those colors, though the secret behind a perfect bouquet all comes down to the style of dress you are wearing. Bring a photo of your dress to the florist and describe the kind of look you want. Do you want something trendy, romantic, or classic? You can find more information about bouquets and flowers on pages 75–85 in this book.

PRESERVE YOUR BOUQUET

If you don't want to toss your bouquet, there are many ways to preserve it as a keepsake after the wedding.

⋙ Preserve the bouquet at a professional florist. That way it will stay close to its original state. Be sure to ask in advance as not all florists offer this service.

⋙ Dry the bouquet by hanging it upside down in a dark place. If you spray the bouquet with hair spray it will remain dust free for longer.

⋙ Select a few of the flowers to press and frame.

The green sprawling bouquet is perfect for the curvaceous bride. A drop-shaped bouquet is suitable for a tall bride, and a round bouquet works best for a petite bride.

THE HAIRDO

A HAIRDO is a piece of art that is truly one of a kind. Keep an open mind when you're sitting in the salon chair on your wedding day, but make sure that you and your hairdresser are on the same page. Hairdos can be varied endlessly—ask yourself if you want it tight or loose, complex or simplistic. The most important things are for the hairdo to feel right for your personality and for you to be comfortable in it.

Make sure you book your appointment well ahead of time. It's always nice to set up a consultation about a month before the wedding where you and the hairdresser talk about your expectations. That way you can make sure you're both on the same page and can even try out some variations. Sometimes this will cost a little extra, while other times it's included in the price of the bridal hair package. Ask for an estimate and make sure you know what is included in the price.

Not all hairdressers are trained in doing bridal hair, so ask for a recommendation from your regular hairdresser. Designing a bridal hairdo is more complicated than you might think, as you must ensure it can survive anything from wind to rain.

HAIR CARE FOR THE BIG DAY

If you want to color or highlight your hair for your wedding, you should do this at least one week before, so you can fix any problems that might occur. Hair that has been dyed the day before can even stain the dress if the air is humid or if it rains.

Condition your hair regularly the last month before your wedding.

Trim your hair about two weeks before the wedding.

If you plan to add highlights, don't do this too close to the wedding day. Hair that has just been highlighted can easily look streaky, so instead do this a week before the wedding.

RELAXED HAIRDO

Falling freely either completely or partially. This has become more and more popular in the last couple of years and can be completed with a veil and tiara. Free-flowing hair gives off a soft and natural impression and looks best if you have long hair.

ACCESSORIES AND HAIR DECORATIONS

The number of hair accessories available has exploded in recent years. Enhance your hair with anything from a simple flower or a miniature bouquet to a gemstone clip, tiara, or crepe.

UPDOS

Updos are still the most popular choice among brides. Styles can vary from strict and intricate to simple and retro. Usually, they'll require you to have a bit of length to your hair, but with professional help and weaves, even brides with short hair can achieve an intricate updo.

MAKEUP

⫸ Don't forget your nails! A manicure and pedicure will do wonders for a complete look.

⫸ Waterproof mascara is recommended for the wedding day.

ON YOUR WEDDING DAY, it is important to use high-quality makeup that will last throughout the day. A good foundation will give you the best possible results. Get facials regularly before the wedding and avoid using new, unknown brands that may cause skin irritation on the wedding day. A classic look is usually preferred—try out different makeup styles ahead of time and make a guide of the order in which each item should be applied.

Figure out whether you want to apply your own makeup or have a professional makeup artist do it for you. It's natural to be stressed and nervous on your wedding day and it can make your hands unsteady and shaky. If you choose to apply your own makeup it can be a good idea to have a friend or bridesmaid there to help you.

If you pick someone else to do your makeup, be sure to explain to him or her what style you want for your day. Do a test run a month before the wedding to make sure that both you and the makeup artist are on the same page.

CHOOSING THE RIGHT ACCESSORIES

YOUR CHOICE OF SHOES AND JEWELRY will create a personal look, but it is easy for the costs to get out of hand. Focus on a few favorites that matter most to you and make sure to budget appropriately. On pages 173–177 you can read more about the rings.

Shoes

If there is ever a time to invest in a pair of expensive shoes, this is it. Spend some extra time and money to find the perfect pair, because they can be the factor that determines whether you have an enjoyable reception or if your feet will be in pain all night. Brand name shoes are often well made and have a better design for your feet than what you will find in the discount stores.

It has become common to wear dainty shoes with high heels and open toes, but remember that you need to be able to wear the shoes all day. With a long gown, brides usually choose shoes with a lower heel and covered toes; after all, they will barely be seen under the dress—at most, only a glimpse of a toe will be revealed. If you wear a short dress, there is more of a reason to wear high heels and open toed shoes.

Also, make sure to have broken in your shoes well beforehand to avoid any blisters during the wedding day. A useful home remedy is to put on wet socks while wearing the shoes to break them in—that way, the shoes get damp and shape around your foot as they dry. However, this is not recommended for shoes with water-sensitive materials, such as silk, since they can stain from the moisture. If you want to use the shoes again after your wedding, it can be a good idea to ask if they can be dyed a different color.

Your feet will thank you if you change into more comfortable shoes when you have an opportunity. You may be able to do so during the ride to the reception hall or during dinner.

A pair of classic shoes can be made into party shoes by just adding a cute detail such as a bow or a pretty clasp.

Choose Your Shoes with Care!

⫸ When you choose your shoes, there are several things to keep in mind to find the perfect pair. Let shoe shape, heel height, and color steer your choice and then find a pair that suits your personal style.

⫸ Don't just buy the first pair you see, but rather choose carefully. Try on, try on, and try on some more!

⫸ Be careful when choosing the height of the heel since you have to be able to move around easily in them all day and all night. If you still insist on a high-heeled pair of shoes, practice walking in them. Start practicing a couple of weeks before the wedding.

⫸ Buy your shoes in the afternoon when your feet are at their most swollen to minimize the risk of buying shoes that are too small.

⫸ Bring a second, more comfortable pair of shoes so you can change during the evening.

WHICH STYLE SUITS YOU BEST?

The classic bridal shoe with a low heel and pointy toe ensures that the dress is pushed forward so you won't trip on the lining.

The bride who does not like heels can choose a very simple style. A pair of flats with beautiful details, such as embroidery or gemstones, enhances the festive feeling.

If you want to be extra trendy, you can buy a pair of modern pumps that fit your color scheme. These shoes can also be worn after the wedding day.

If you are looking for a glamorous style, go for a pair of classic pumps with an eye-catching clasp and gemstones.

This model exudes an airier feel, but it is steady thanks to the cut of the heel. The high heel does, however, require good balance.

A shoe with an open toe, also called a "peep toe," requires a flawless pedicure.

If your shoe size is right in between two sizes, choose a shoe with an ankle strap. This will prevent you from slipping out of your shoes on the dance floor.

Even if you're used to walking in high heels, it will strain your feet to walk in them all day long. Your feet are better off if you choose heels that are slightly lower than what you would usually wear.

The kitten heel is suitable for brides who are not used to walking in heels. This style can also be easily adjusted because of the ankle strap.

Slingbacks are not a classic wedding shoe choice and will require a perfect pedicure. They are not very steady and will require good balance and stable ankles.

Bear in mind that shoes become a focal point when you wear a shorter dress—go for a more exciting style.

Umbrella

Rain is considered good luck on your wedding day, but no bride wants to look like a drowned rat! Invest in a beautiful white parasol that can protect you from rain and powerful sun rays. It's also a pretty accessory for your wedding pictures.

Bag

No matter how prepared you are, you can still end up with last-minute surprises on your wedding day, and a well-stocked purse can be your savior. If the bag ends up getting too heavy, you can hand it over to one of your bridesmaids.

>> Match your shoes and bag to the dress. Or why not pick your theme color and it's complement?

SUPER IMPORTANT TO HAVE IN YOUR BAG!
- Blister band-aids
- Regular band-aids
- Safety pins
- Krazy glue
- Tape
- Makeup for touch ups throughout the evening
- Nail polish or glue for fake nails
- Painkillers
- A second pair of pantyhose
- Hair pins and hair spray
- Something sweet to prevent low blood sugar

Veil

Not everyone chooses to wear a veil, but many feel that it is the clearest way to distinguish oneself as the bride. If you choose to wear a veil, be sure to choose a style and color that matches your dress and complements the shape of your face. Also remember that your choice of hairstyle will be limited by the veil, so be sure to tell your stylist that you will be wearing one.

The veil can either be attached high up on the crown of your head or further down on your neck, and if you want you can always ask your hairstylist to attach it loosely to make it easier to remove after the wedding ceremony.

Hair Accessories

In addition to the veil, there are plenty of hair accessories to choose from, for example a tiara, headband, or diadem, and decorations such as gemstones, pearls, or flowers. When picking the accessory, keep in mind what kind of hairstyle you'll have and what suits you and your style.

A hair decoration or veil is an effective way to frame your face and tie the look together.

UNDERGARMENTS

⇛ Is your dress a bit see-through in certain lighting? Choose smooth, nude colored lingerie to wear during the day so it doesn't show.

A BEAUTIFUL BRIDE begins with her undergarments, and there is special-made underwear intended to be worn under a wedding dress. Most commonly, brides wear sleek, light colored—often nude—underwear, but these are more practical than beautiful. It's a good idea to have two sets of underwear: practical for the day and lingerie for the evening. For best results, begin with a bra style and size that fits you and your dress. If the dress is sleeveless, you will need a strapless bra.

It is quite common for brides to order wedding dresses that are slightly too small in the hopes of losing weight before the ceremony. If this doesn't happen, a lace-up corset is a good solution if there is not enough time to alter the dress.

FOR UNDERNEATH THE DRESS

Here are some tips on choosing undergarments:

⇛ Wash and try on. When you have found the perfect underwear, you should wash it according to the instructions and then try them on again. That way, you'll know if they have shrunk or expanded after the wash.

⇛ Thigh highs or pantyhose? Discreetly nude or white? Options are plentiful so consider what you like most and don't forget to buy an extra pair.

⇛ Avoid seams! Besides the shape, remember that underwear should not be visible through the dress. Be practical when choosing daywear and go for sexier lingerie for the nighttime.

Choose practical undergarments for daywear and switch to sexy lingerie for the wedding night.

Garter belts can be sexy to wear, but are time-consuming when visiting the restroom, and you also risk the seams being visible through the dress. Save yourself the trouble and wear them for the wedding night instead.

Choose the Right Bra

Your choice of bra depends entirely on your style of dress. Here are some of the most common styles:

MULTIFUNCTION. Certain bras have straps that can be removed or adjusted. Choose this style if you are wearing a halter dress, for example.

STRAPLESS. A strapless dress naturally requires a strapless bra. If you have a large cup size, it is important to find a bra that offers extra support.

BUSTIER. If you are wearing a dress with delicate fabric, it is a good idea to choose a bustier. It shapes both your waist and bust and you eliminate any sharp edges that can be seen through a delicate dress.

INVISIBLE. Do you have a revealing or tight-fitting dress and a small- or a medium-sized chest? Then it might be best for you to wear an invisible bra that you can attach to the bust with tape.

MULTIFUNCTION

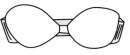

STRAPLESS

BUSTIER

Garter

These days, it's very common for the bride to wear a garter. It was originally meant to keep the stockings from falling down instead of wearing the traditional garter belt. In the United States, it is traditional for the groom to toss the garter, and it's supposed to bring good luck in love for the bachelor who catches it. A garter can be a beautiful and fun accessory to wear under the dress, but make sure it is not unflattering to your overall shape if you're wearing a tight-fitting dress.

INVISIBLE

PETTICOAT FOR A MORE FLATTERING SHAPE

≫ Wearing a petticoat under the dress can make a big difference and helps your dress get the right shape, especially if it has a full skirt. Choose a petticoat in tulle or crinoline for maximum volume. If you are wearing a sleek chiffon dress, however, you should choose a tight slip that shapes and flattens. Many times a petticoat is included with the dress, but sometimes you have to pay extra for it. Check with your store.

THE BRIDEGROOM

From Suits to Tuxedos

Even though the spotlight is primarily on the bride during the wedding day, the bridegroom is just as important. Your choice of clothing will mostly depend on two things: how formal your wedding will be and who you are. In earlier times, the men dressed in the best suit they had, and if they did not have one, they borrowed from a friend or relative. In some instances they would even borrow one from their priest. Today, it is rather a question of if you want to marry formally or as casually as possible. It is important to decide this early on when you send out invitations so guests will know what to wear.

SUIT

ARE YOU CONSIDERING getting married in a suit? If you are, you're in good company. Today, the suit is the obvious uniform for western men and one of the most elegant things you can wear. Originally, the suit consisted of three pieces—pants, jacket, and vest—all from the same fabric. These days, the vest has pretty much become obsolete since the temperatures in the west have increased and there is really no need for an extra layer in our current environment. For weddings, the most common suit colors are navy blue, dark gray, or black. In the summer it is also common to use a sleek, light beige suit.

The suit should have two or three buttons per row. More or fewer just look ridiculous. It is up to you to choose a single- or double-breasted suit. For less formal settings and among close friends it is okay to have the single-breasted suit open, but the general rule is to always keep it buttoned up. Wearing a double-breasted suit open, however, is one of the seven deadly sins!

Suit pants are made of the same fabric as the suit jacket. Whether or not you want creases in your pants is a matter of taste, but if you are tall it's a good idea to have the pants creased. If you're shorter, you should definitely avoid creases.

A clean, conservative cotton shirt is preferable to a trendy, colored one. The most elegant way to wear it is with French cuffs. As you probably know, French cuffs demand cuff links, which offer a chance for you to shine. The collar should be of classic cut or a cutaway with wide-spread points (read more about collars on page 160). Avoid button down and tab collars for weddings.

(read more about collars on page 160)

SUIT AND TIE DRESS CODE

For formal events such as weddings, invitations often mention suit and tie as the dress code. This does not mean blazers in various colors and a pair of pants in any style you choose, but rather a complete suit and tie.

ABSOLUTELY FORBIDDEN!

Whatever you do, do not button the last button of the suit. This rule stems from the late nineteenth century when Edward VII couldn't button his last button because of his potbelly. The noblemen followed suit and soon after it was a worldwide tradition.

Accessories

A turtleneck might be stylish to wear with a suit, but for weddings, it is best to wear a button down shirt with an attractive tie instead.

A suit looks more elegant with a pocket square or a boutonnière on the left lapel. Black socks that reach fairly high up the calf are a must—forget about the white tube socks. Forget, too, the cool chunky belt with metal studs. If you have to wear a belt, it should be a thin one. The belt should match the shoes. If you are wearing a blue, gray, or black suit, the shoes should obviously be black and polished with a thin leather sole, and make sure the heel is not worn down unevenly.

If your dress code is "black suit" on your invitation, keep in mind that this dress code is formal and will require a tie. There are plenty of fabrics to choose from, and the tie can be either in a solid color or striped or even a discreet polka dot pattern. A silk tie with a Windsor knot is a safe choice. If you want to stand out and be a little more original you can choose the classic four-in-hand knot, which breaks up the look with its asymmetry.

WHITE TIE

AROUND 1870, white tie became the most elegant of dress codes for men, and ever since it has served as the most formal dress code of all. White tie does not leave much room for experimentation—actually, there's none at all—so if you choose to send out invitations to a white tie wedding, it's best that you know white tie etiquette.

First and foremost, a white tie jacket is always black. The jacket has silk lapels and the pants have side stripes in the same material. The jacket is not meant to be buttoned up, and you must wear a white handkerchief in your breast pocket, folded according to your own choice (see suggestions for folding options on pages 163–164). The pants do not have creases or belt loops, and are instead held up by thin, white suspenders. Make sure that the length of your pants is correct when you rent or buy your white tie ensemble. They absolutely cannot be long enough to crumple at the bottom by the shoes. The length of the pants can be altered slightly by adjusting your suspenders. Long black socks, preferably silk, are recommended as well as thin, black, patent leather shoes with a low heel.

The classic shirt for white tie is always white with a starched chest and preferably made of piqué. The cuffs are simple and are buttoned up with loose buttons, just like at the chest and neck. Over the shirt you wear a white vest, but unlike the suit vest, you should button all the buttons. The bottom of the vest is meant to show by half an inch under the jacket. Finally, you have one choice to make: you can choose between a single-breasted or a double-breasted vest.

For a white tie event, you are required to wear a white bowtie, which is tied over the stand up or wing collar. When outside, the white tie look is complemented by a top hat and a white silk scarf—and if you want to look elegant in a vintage manner, you can also choose to wear a cloak instead of a coat.

Rent or Buy?

There is no reason whatsoever to buy a white tie outfit for one single wedding. It's only worth the investment if you are planning on attending several white tie affairs. If you rent a white tie ensemble, make sure that all buttons are included along with instructions on how to use them. Note that the pants are meant to have six buttons for the suspenders, and check that the number of shirt and vest buttons are correct.

HELP GETTING DRESSED

⫸ Try on your clothes a day or two before the wedding and expect the dressing part to take at least half an hour. Ideally, the best man or a groomsman should help you. The buttons are the most complicated part; even if modern shirts have regular buttons, they will most likely have three loose pearl buttons, and the cuffs are held together by loose buttons as well. The suspenders are also fastened by buttons—six of them!

⫸ This dress-code has many names: white tie, tailsuit, top hat and tails, full evening dress, habit, habit franc, habit noir, or grand tenue depending on where in the world you live.

TUXEDO

ARE YOU CONSIDERING wearing a tuxedo to your wedding? Then you should read this first. It is said that the tuxedo was invented in 1885 by the ultimate party prince, the Duke of Windsor. The item quickly became a trend in the United States, where the name "tuxedo" was born. The tuxedo was intended as a dinner jacket, worn for evening entertainment such as cocktail parties and in certain cases for dinners of the more cheerful character. The tuxedo was essentially used for the complete opposite of formal events and according to tradition, should not be worn for weddings.

If you do want to wear a tuxedo for your wedding, it should be black or midnight blue, unless it is a summer event held outside, on a boat, or in the tropics, where the tuxedo jacket can then be white. The pants have silk stripes and the jacket has a silk-covered shawl collar or silk-covered lapels. The complementing bowtie and pants are always black, as are the shoes. Keep in mind that tuxedos are only worn in the evening, never before five o'clock.

Accessories

The tuxedo is worn with a sash, or cummerbund as it is more commonly known. The use of a cummerbund originates in India and is an old tradition. Originally, it was used to show which clan you belonged to, but it also was used during formal military events. Today, the cummerbund is used in military events all over the world, for covering the break between pants and shirt. In comparison to the always-black bowtie, the cummerbund can be in any color or pattern. The folds are worn upward, as pockets used to be sewn into them.

Belts are not used with tuxedos, but you can definitely wear suspenders. The shirt should always be white with French cuffs, and cufflinks are a standard requirement. If you want to make it even more fancy, you can choose buttons that match the cufflinks. The pocket square is white and of the finest cotton. It goes without saying that you should tie your own bowtie and never buy a clip on.

BOWTIE COLORS

If it says black tie dinner, tuxedo, or cravat noir on the invitation, it means that a tuxedo is required without exception. The terms indicate the color of the tie, which should be black, no matter what color the tuxedo jacket is.

CUTAWAY

IF YOU WANT to dress a little bit more originally on your wedding day, the cutaway (or morning coat) is a great alternative. The cutaway can be described as a mix of a redingote (see below) and white tie. It is more formal than suit and tie, but less formal than white tie. The jacket is long and diagonally cut with tails and should be black, though a gray jacket is acceptable. The pants are often gray or gray striped, or alternatively, black. The item is perfectly suited for daytime wear and is never worn after 6 p.m.

Traditionalists wear a gray vest, a white shirt, and a gray tie or a gray ascot under the cutaway. If you want to be more contemporary, you can alter the colors of the vest and ascot to any color you like, although light colors are the most common. The shoes should be black, the gloves gray, and the top hat gray or black. The outfit is a must for horseracing events at Royal Ascot in England and are complemented by the women's elaborate hats.

TIE AN ASCOT

1. Begin by arranging one end so that it hangs six inches lower than the other.

2. Cross the longer end over the shorter end and place it behind.

3. Bring it around for one full turn.

4. Pull the end up behind the knot.

5. Let the top end hang loose over the other.

6. Adjust the knot under the upper end.

REDINGOTE

TODAY, SWEDISH PLAYWRIGHT August Strindberg's favorite manner of dress is nearly extinct. In the United States, it can be very difficult to find, so perhaps this is a choice to consider if you are getting married abroad. The redingote—which was in fashion during the 1800s—is a kind of long blazer that can be worn both indoors and out. In comparison to the tailcoat, the redingote is cut in straight lines, but it does have a split tail in the back to accommodate horse riding. The material can vary from black wool to colored silk. A redingote is worn with a vest, white shirt, tie, or ascot with black shoes and pants.

Cutaways are only used for daytime weddings, never at night. Here is a sober cutaway in gray complemented by an apricot-colored boutonnière.

FROCK COAT

THE FROCK COAT is a great alternative if you want an outfit that's fancier and more fun than a suit, but you're not comfortable sending invitations for a white tie event. This is also a kind of long jacket, slightly shorter than a redingote, and it can be found in all imaginable variations.

Originally, the frock coat was always black, but these days you can also find styles reminiscent of the classic Beatles album *Sgt. Pepper's Lonely Hearts Club Band*. The frock coat is often paisley patterned in a colored silk with a so-called Nehru collar—a small stand-up collar rather than lapels. This is usually paired with black pants and a vest. The vest is also often in paisley-patterned colored silk; however, it's usually in a different color than the jacket. The most common thing is to complement it with an ascot or a shirt with Nehru collar, which of course can never be worn with a regular tie.

Clothing for the Bridegroom

SUIT AND TIE

WHITE TIE

TUXEDO

CUTAWAY

REDINGOTE

FROCK COAT

OVERCOAT

THE SHIRT

EVEN THOUGH THE MODERN dress shirt was not created until 1871—at the same time as the first shirt with a fully buttoned chest was registered—the white shirt was already long established as a component of the successful man's attire. Although it was acceptable to wear striped shirts for everyday wear, these were never acceptable for formal occasions as they could possibly hide dirt or spots. Perhaps this is the reason why a white shirt is still considered nicer than a patterned one?

The actual shape of the shirt has been fine-tuned over the years, but essentially no dramatic change has been made since World War I. The breast pocket was added during the 1960s, but it really doesn't serve any function; it was simply added as a detail when men stopped wearing vests with their suits.

Even though the suit will stay on during the whole reception, the choice of shirt is more important than many realize, and the most important detail of the shirt is the collar.

For a cutaway, you can choose either a stand-up collar or a turn down one. A turn down collar is the safest bet, but no matter what collar you choose, the shirt should always have a pleated chest with hidden or exposed buttoning. If you choose exposed buttons, you should use loose buttons that match the cuff links you have chosen to hold the French cuffs together. The most elegant shirt is a cotton piqué.

The shirt for white tie events is always white with piqué chest and stand-up collar and is buttoned with cufflinks even though it has single cuffs. Keep in mind that this is a little tricky to put on—make sure you reserve some extra time to get dressed. The white-tie shirt is matched with a white tie and vest. Without tie and vest, this shirt can also be worn with a tailcoat.

Elegant is the first word that comes to mind when describing the tuxedo shirt. It has French cuffs where even the top buttons are closed, but has loose buttons and a pleated chest. A traditional tuxedo shirt has a standard folded collar, not a stand-up collar. Even this shirt can be a little tricky to put on, so make sure you have some extra time to get dressed. The shirt is paired with a black bowtie that you tie yourself.

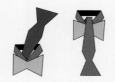
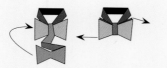
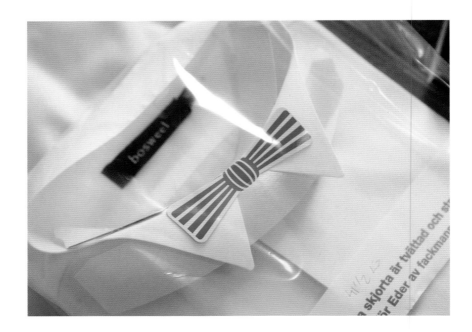

The Shape of the Collar and Its Function

For more than a hundred years, the biggest variations in shirts have been the collars. Up until the 1930s, the stand-up collar dominated, but when more and more men started wearing ties rather than ascots, the folded collar had its major breakthrough. The three most common collars are: turn-down collar, cut-away collar, and button-down collar.

TURN-DOWN COLLAR. A discreet, formal, and a very classic collar. Is suitable for thinner tie knots such as "four-in-hand." The top buttonholes are closed with loose buttons, which makes it suitable for a tuxedo with a shawl collar.

CUTAWAY COLLAR. A comfortable side-spreading collar, which is just as iconically English as gin and tonic. The collar offers room for a large Windsor knot and is used with suits or cutaway coats. The collar is also called a spread collar.

BUTTON-DOWN COLLAR. Is definitely not used for weddings! This collar was created when polo players got tired of their collars flapping. The sports connection forbids this collar from being used for formal events. It also looks nicest without any tie at all.

The Cuffs

These days, cuffs usually have buttons attached, but for festive occasions the classic French cuffs are always nicer; these are closed by loose buttons. They are definitely the nicest looking ones. One exception, however, is the tuxedo shirt, which is always closed with cufflinks, but only has a single cuff.

Material and Quality

Cotton of the highest quality is a must for a formal shirt. You can determine the quality of a shirt by the thread count of the fabric—the thinner the fabric and the better the quality, the softer the shirt will be. The shirt is meant to be slim enough to fit well under the suit, and you should be able to move around comfortably. The collar shouldn't be so tight that you feel strangled when fastening the top button, but it is also not meant to be so loose that it shifts around.

≫ Consider asking your best man to help you with the cufflinks.

ABSOLUTELY FORBIDDEN!

≫ Short sleeved shirt and tie with a suit. This is unacceptable and many men who do this should know better. You simply do not walk into a wedding in a short-sleeved shirt, no matter how hot it is.

≫ Patterned shirts. No Hawaiian or checkered shirts. When it comes to baby blue, pink, and striped shirts with white cuffs and collar, you will have to judge on your own if you think it is suitable, but the safest bet is always to wear a white shirt.

≫ Taking off your suit jacket. Have you heard of the word "nightshirt?" It explains why once upon a time the shirt was an item to sleep in. With that in mind, it is a given that you never take off your suit jacket.

≫ Things in your breast pocket. Salesmen, doctors, and pilots are the most common professionals who break this rule. Worst-case scenario, you will end up with permanent stains from a ballpoint pen.

≫ Button-down collar. The buttons on the collar have a past tied to sports and are not considered suitable for formal events.

CHOOSE THE RIGHT ACCESSORIES

ENDLESS INSTRUCTIONS have been written about wedding dresses and their accessories, but the groom's options are seldom mentioned. Few know that the choice of attire is steered by both the clothing's history and rules for what can be combined with what.

Boutonnière

Many men know the boutonnière, or button hole, as the flower they wore on their tuxedo to match their prom date's corsage. For weddings, the boutonnière is a flower the groom wears on his left lapel. It is said that originally the flower was picked from the bridal bouquet and was attached to the groom's buttonhole to show his connection to the bride.

The flower can definitely match the bridal bouquet, but there is, of course, flexibility for personal taste. If the groom has his own entourage with groomsmen, they can wear the same flower as the groom, but a smaller version. The boutonnière can be anything from a small, cut flower attached to the buttonhole to a small masterpiece or miniature bouquet arranged by the same florist who arranged the bridal bouquet.

Pocket Squares

The handkerchief is an elegant accessory to keep in the breast pocket of the jacket and is not meant for blowing your nose with. At formal events you should always have a handkerchief in your breast pocket of your tuxedo or tailcoat. The best choice is to fold it into points or with a thin ribbon for the Presidential fold. Avoid carrying a Puff fold with a tuxedo.

THREE-POINT FOLD. Unfold the handkerchief and place it so that a corner is pointed upward and another corner is pointed downward. Fold the handkerchief in half by placing the left corner on top of the right. Then fold the bottom corner so it is placed about half an inch to the right of the upper corner. Then fold the right corner straight across to the left. Finally, fold the bottom part so that the handkerchief fits perfectly in the breast pocket.

THE PRESIDENTIAL FOLD. The way James Bond wears his pocket square. Unfold the handkerchief and fold the left edge towards the middle of it, then fold the right edge so the edges to meet in the middle. Repeat the same procedure so that the handkerchief's top and bottom edges meet in the middle. Adjust so about half an inch of the handkerchief is exposed at the breast pocket.

THE PUFF FOLD. Unfold the handkerchief, grab in the middle, and lift it like you're a magician. Fold neatly at the bottom and hide the edges. Adjust so it fills up the pocket nicely. It is meant to look like it was placed there casually.

Watch

There are not many accessories available for men and perhaps that is why watch brand and style is so important to some; it can be just as important to them as their car. But no matter how nice and expensive your watch may be, you should decide if you really want to wear it on your wedding day. It can be considered rude to look at your watch during a wedding, no matter if it is your own or your friend's.

For suit and tie, you can wear a wristwatch, but it should be a discreet model. However, you should never wear a watch when wearing a tuxedo. Only pocket watches, which are attached to the vest, are acceptable.

>>> A pocket watch is the most proper no matter what you are wearing. Wearing a wristwatch to a wedding can seem a little disrespectful toward the wedding couple. When you are at a wedding, there is no need to keep track of time!

Cufflinks

A nice pair of cufflinks should be a part of every man's wardrobe and make a perfect present, no matter if they are a gift for someone or for yourself.

There are really no direct rules when it comes to cufflinks. If the shirt is intended to be buttoned with regular buttons, they will be attached on a single cuff. If the shirt has French cuffs, there will be no buttons attached, but rather just buttonholes that are intended for cufflinks. It's really no more complicated than that.

For cutaway coats, the classic look is to use smooth-surface cufflinks in gold or mother-of-pearl. These can be matched with the same buttons used for the chest area. You can be about as creative as you want to when it comes to the design of the buttons, and there are a plethora of shapes and colors to choose from. The most common thing, however, is to match them to your shirt, tie, and pocket handkerchief to add a touch of color.

AROUND YOUR NECK

TIE, BOWTIE, OR ASCOT? Whatever you choose is just a matter of taste and convention. For certain attire there are requirements—a tuxedo, for example, always requires a black bowtie.

Tie

There are several knots to choose from and certain ones are better suited for certain occasions. Here are two classics:

FOUR-IN-HAND KNOT. This classic knot is one of the oldest and hails from the mid-1800s. The knot is somewhat smaller and less regular in shape than the symmetrical, triangular Windsor knot.

WINDSOR KNOT. Edward VII, the Duke of Windsor, was known as the "Fashion King" but it's a myth that he invented the Windsor knot. The Windsor knot is most suitable first and foremost for its size. It is ideal for thin silk ties and for collars with widely placed tips.

Bowtie

The dress code for tuxedo is labeled "Black Tie," indicating the bowtie should always be black. The white bowtie is only used for White Tie attire, as the dress code states. The bowtie is meant to be tied on your own for the most fashion points (see page 160). It is best to practice beforehand, because it is not easy.

Ascot

The modern ascot was created at the end of the 1800s when men started tying their ties in a more casual way inside the shirt to show that they had left the office. When the ascot later became more common as a formal accessory, it was worn outside a buttoned up shirt.

The knot itself can be compared to a half-finished knot on a regular tie. It looks best if you tie the ascot on your own (see page 154).

THE ORIGINS OF THE TIE

There is evidence that men were already tying fabric around their necks in Roman times, and it's not too much of a stretch to suppose that they were doing so long before, partly for warmth and partly to be fashionable. The Croatian army wore artfully tied ties around their necks during the Thirty Years' War. The fashion-forward Frenchmen noticed and imitated the look. *La croate*—the cravat—was born!

SHOES

UNLIKE THE BRIDE, the groom does not necessarily have to buy any special shoes for the wedding. But what kind of shoe is appropriate to wear for the special day?

If you follow tradition, there are a couple of ground rules to follow, such as dark shoes being more suitable than light-colored ones. Avoid wearing brown shoes with a black suit. For a blue suit you can, however, wear either brown or black shoes depending on what time of day it is. Another rule of thumb is that light-colored shoes can be worn during the day but never after 6 p.m.

If you don't own any fancy shoes, this is a perfect opportunity to invest in a great pair, but it will cost you a pretty penny. A pair of great quality men's shoes will last you for the rest of your life.

What Kind of Shoes Go Well with What Attire?

WHITE TIE. Simple. There is only one option here: patent leather shoes.

MORNING DRESS. Since the morning dress is mostly used when outside, you should avoid wearing patent leather shoes. Feel free to combine with a pair of smooth, black shoes of the Oxford or monk model. Avoid jodhpurs, riding boots, and loafers.

REDINGOTE. A classic redingote coat is black and so the shoes should also be black, just like for the morning dress. Patent leather shoes are fine for the reception, but you should not wear them in church.

FROCK COAT. Since these creations can be colored any which way today, black shoes are recommended.

TUXEDO. Many think that you have to wear patent leather shoes with a tuxedo, but this is not the case. It is more appropriate to wear a pair of well-polished thin leather shoes or elegant loafers with a tuxedo.

SUIT. During winter and in the evenings, a dark suit with matching black shoes is preferred. During the summer and during the day you can wear a light-colored suit and light-colored shoes.

BLING

Ring Selection and Jewelry for the Big Day

Genuine pearls, gold, diamonds . . . Your wedding is one of the few occasions when you can pull out your finest jewelry and let yourself shine. The choice of jewelry and what is best suited for your dress code is endless and totally up to your own taste. Try on both antique and new before you decide! Jewelry often becomes nicer with age, so why not shop around at antique stores?

If you want a unique memory for life, perhaps you can order a special-made piece from a jeweler. Pearls to decorate the bride's hair and ears are very popular at weddings and can be combined with a pearl necklace or a chunkier necklace that goes with an open-neck dress.

THE WEDDING BAND

A WEDDING BAND isn't just a piece of jewelry, but is also the ultimate symbol of your love and a visible link between the two of you. You will wear your rings daily—hopefully for the rest of your lives—and therefore you should choose your rings with some thought.

The tradition of exchanging rings goes back a long way and can be found in many places around the world, but how it is done differs from country to country. We think of the man getting down on one knee to propose to the woman with a readymade ring in a box. This is an American tradition, and when the woman agrees, the couple is engaged.

The engagement ring in the United States is traditionally a single diamond, while the actual wedding ring is a simple gold band called a "wedding band" because of its appearance. It used to be common for both the engagement ring and the wedding ring to be smooth and simple and worn together. Even today, there is a greater demand for plain rings for the groom.

Lately, people have started choosing rings that are more personal, and now there are more options for materials, shapes, and even color. There is really no right or wrong, so anything is acceptable. They are your rings and you will be wearing them, not anyone else who might be vocal about the rings you've chosen. The most important thing is that you start looking well in advance and try on various styles to see what you actually like, and if you want to match rings or have individual ones. At a jeweler, you can have your rings created from your own designs; despite what people think, this option is rarely more expensive.

You might be tempted to look online for a deal, but truth be told, it takes a lot of knowledge to know what you're getting online. Find out how the rings have been constructed and what quality stones are used. Precious stones can vary tremendously in quality and each stone differs in durability. The same goes for diamonds. They vary depending on cut, color, and quality, and all of this should be indicated on a certificate that is included in the purchase. Make sure the stones don't come from a country that doesn't uphold human rights laws—if you are unsure, ask for a certificate that assures this.

THE REAL THING?

➤ Always confirm that the ring is genuine and ask for a certificate.

VARIOUS STYLES

➤ Eternity ring. Have several small diamonds in a row on the band.

➤ Solitaire. A smooth ring with one single stone, most often a diamond.

➤ Sidestone ring. Has one larger stone along with two or more smaller stones beside it.

➤ Smooth ring. Many choose a smooth style as a wedding band or engagement ring.

Diamond Quality

In the United States, the engagement ring quality is judged by the "4C" criteria—clarity, color, cut, and carat—and the price for the diamond is set primarily according to their combination. A large, very white, well-polished diamond without any flaws is therefore the most expensive. But what is really behind these criteria?

A common ring combination for women.

CLARITY. The cleaner the diamond is of internal imperfections, called "inclusions," the clearer the diamond and the more durable it will be, and it will have a better possibility of reflecting light. The most common classifications are VVS, VS, and SI, where the first mentioned means the least inclusions of the three.

This ring is called an eternity ring.

COLOR. A completely colorless diamond appears to be really white, and the whiter it is the more expensive it is. With lesser color quality, the diamond will appear more yellow. The color scale for diamonds has nine steps. The highest quality is called River (R), which is the definition of a stone with a rare, white color. Thereafter, the color scale goes from Top Wesselton (rare white), Wesselton (white), Top Crystal (very white toned), Crystal (lightly white toned), Top Cape (white toned), Cape (lightly yellow toned), Light Yellow (light yellow), and lastly, Yellow, which is obviously yellow in color. There are also colored diamonds, such as pink and black, but the color scale is not used for these diamonds.

Diamonds are not the only precious stones out there.

CUT. This criteria is about the shape of the diamond, in part how well cut it is. The better the cut, the brighter the diamond. The most common shapes are round, princess, baguette, and cushion cut, which is a square cut without the sharp corners.

CARAT. The carat (Ct) for diamonds is not the same as carat for gold (K), but is rather a measurement of mass for the stone. Remember that the price of a diamond rises faster than the size of the diamond when it increases in carat.

For a long time, smooth rings in red gold were the most popular choice.

Find the Rings of Your Dreams

To find your dream rings, you should spend a lot of time trying on various styles to see how they fit your hands. It is not necessary for your rings to match; instead, make sure both of you are happy with your choices and remember that you will wear your rings on an everyday basis. If you want to wear the engagement and wedding rings together, make sure to try them on to see if they fit together. Here, you should pay attention to choice of metal, width, and height, which are important to take into consideration. Do not forget to order your inscriptions for each other's names and wedding date. Perhaps you want to engrave a symbol or write a few choice words on the inside or outside of the ring. Before the wedding, it can be a good idea to polish your engagement ring so it looks as new as the wedding bands.

>>> Choose the right size. Ring size is set in various ways depending on the country. If you are planning on buying your rings abroad, you can find size conversions on the Internet. Keep in mind that one's fingers often swell when it's hot outside and shrink when it gets cold.

>>> Take care of your rings. To keep your jewelry shiny, you have to take care of them and clean them. Use water and a few drops of soap on a soft toothbrush to clean the rings. Also, ask your jeweler to make sure that the stones are securely fastened every so often.

*A tip for the bride is to bring along several styles of jewelry when wedding dress shopping. The jewelry makes
a big difference. Do the same when trying out hairstyles. For the groom, it comes down to nothing more
than a watch and the most important item—the wedding band.*

THE WEDDING GIFT

THE WEDDING GIFT is a time-honored gesture that you may wish to participate in, and it's most common for the groom to give his wife a piece of jewelry. Presenting the wedding gift to the new bride on the morning after the wedding day is an old tradition, which originally was meant as a pension or insurance for the woman, consisting of money or property. This was given because a woman did not automatically inherit her husband's property if he passed away before she did; to ensure that she would not be kicked out of their house by the person who did inherit, the wife was often given the house and its surrounding land as a gift in order to survive. The gift, however, was not necessarily a gift of ownership, but rather a right of disposal for the remainder of the bride's life. The gift would be reversed if the widow remarried or died.

In the 1700s, it became more common to give the bride a piece of jewelry in the form of a locket, which held a picture or a lock of hair from the husband inside of it. These days, the wedding gift varies and it's even common for a bride to give her husband a gift. A ring to put on your right hand is a common wedding gift for both husband and wife.

JEWELRY

A necklace is the most common wedding gift from husband to wife. Choosing a wedding gift for your husband can be a bit trickier, but a pair of elegant cufflinks is never wrong!

A wedding gift does not have to be expensive, but try to make it personal.

THE RECEPTION

An Evening to Remember

You don't get many opportunities to invite your friends and family to a big party. The wedding reception is one of the biggest highlights of your lives, and putting on a grand celebration will give your friends a chance to show their happiness and share in your love in the best way possible.

No matter if you want a formal sit down dinner with plenty of speeches or if you choose to have a picnic in the park, this is something really fun to plan together. The type of reception will depend in part on your budget— most people have to compromise in order to stay within budget. Carefully consider what you think makes for a successful reception and use that to create your personal celebration. Everyone is there to celebrate you and so it should be on your terms and just as you want it.

FIND THE BEST RECEPTION HALL

THE RECEPTION HALL SETS THE TONE for the kind of event you want to have and is one of the first things to consider when you start planning your wedding. It is common to offer a three-course meal at a wedding reception at a more formal venue. If you choose to hold the reception in a garden out in the countryside, you may be able to have a more casual dress code for the day.

When you have chosen what kind of reception you want, it is time to start looking for the perfect venue. Take a look at several locations that suit your needs and then ask for quotes to see what will be included and at what price. To avoid any unpleasant surprises, there are a few questions you should have answered before you decide on the venue.

SIGN A CONTRACT!

Ask for a signed contract of all the things you have agreed upon, including price. If you book far in advance, it is especially a good idea. Then you won't have any unpleasant surprises or price increases.

- Is the reception hall close to the wedding venue? If not, you need to inform your wedding guests if you are arranging for transportation or if they will have to get there on their own.

- Are you considering cooking your own food? Check if this is allowed. Certain places offer catering and will not allow outside food to be brought in. This may even apply to the wedding cake—don't forget to ask specifically about this.

- Bringing your own alcohol instead of buying it straight from the restaurant can reduce the budget considerably, but not all places will allow this. Double check on the liquor license rules if you plan on charging your guests for the alcohol.

- When will you have access to the venue? If you are planning on decorating it yourselves, it would be nice to be able to do this the day before.

- Is cleaning included? Sometimes there is a separate cleaning fee, which is not always optional. If you want to handle the cleanup on your own, you should find out who in your circle is willing to help. Set clear time frames to avoid contention at the end of the day.

- When do you have to clear out from the venue? Make sure someone close to you is responsible for returning the key and taking care of returning the security deposit to you, so you don't have to get up early the next day.

25 Tips for a Successful Reception

1.

Have a table available where your guests can place the wedding gifts.

2.

Create a pretty box for envelopes with financial contributions
so they don't get misplaced.

3.

Check on ventilation and heat to make sure the temperature
is appropriate for the weather.

4.

If you have hired a photographer, you should make sure that the toastmaster or MC has planned breaks for him or her to eat so you don't risk
losing photo opportunities during any speeches.

5.

Place ashtrays outside the entrance if some of your guests are smokers.

6.

Create a general schedule for the toastmaster to follow.

7.

Designate someone to be responsible for transportation between
wedding and reception venues.

8.

Have you booked a live band? Be sure to check well ahead of time that
all speakers and microphones in the reception hall are working.

9.

Set out blank CDs with stamped envelopes. That way, your guests can
send you the pictures they took of you during the day.

10.

Bring comfortable shoes to change into for the evening if you
are worried about blisters.

11.

Place water pitchers on the dinner tables. It helps limit both wine con-
sumption and drunkenness amongst the guests.

12.

Purchase a guest book with a matching pen. Ask the toastmaster or MC
to pass it around during the reception so everyone has a chance to sign
it for you.

13.
Check that there is enough space on the dance floor for dancing.

14.
Ask someone to push aside the tables when it is time to dance.

15.
Set a vase on the head table where you can place your bridal bouquet.

16.
Ask someone, preferably the host couple or the venue coordinator, to keep track of the restrooms to ensure they are fresh and clean and that there is toilet paper available.

17.
If there are only paper towels in the restrooms, bring your own cotton towels to hang up to make it more comfortable.

18.
Clearly state on your invitations that requests for speeches have to be submitted beforehand so you won't have any spontaneous speeches given by drunken guests.

19.
Give the kitchen specific information about allergies and other special food requests.

20.
Find out in advance how big the refrigerator is to make sure all your food can fit if you are planning on bringing your own.

21.
The importance of checklists deserves to be repeated. You should even specify who does what.

22.
Have several non-alcoholic options available. Drinking water all evening is not that much fun. Create a special drink for the day!

23.
If children will attend, it might be a good idea to assign a play area so parents and other guests will have some peace and adult conversation.

24.
Prepare a lovely basket in the restroom with miscellaneous emergency items for guests, such as pantyhose, pain killers, tampons, and band-aids.

25.
Dedicate a page in the program to miscellaneous information, such as where the restrooms are located and phone numbers of local taxi companies.

SUCCEED WITH YOUR SEATING ARRANGEMENTS

THE SEATING ARRANGEMENT IS USUALLY the most complicated nut to crack, but if you succeed, you will have all the potential for a successful reception. Start early on this puzzle so you have enough time to tweak it throughout the planning. There are two options for a great seating arrangement: you either break all the rules and place the guests the way you prefer or you go strictly by the book and use the traditional rules of seating etiquette.

Seating Etiquette

The wedding couple sits at the head table. One option is to sit the close family at this table as well. According to traditional seating etiquette, the close family sits nearest the wedding couple. The basic hierarchy for this type of seating is according to relationship first and according to age second. Sometimes it can be difficult to manage an arrangement that feels right and in those cases it might be a good idea to break tradition.

These days, families can come in many different forms and it can be difficult for the wedded couple to know how to place divorced parents' new partners. If everyone gets along with one another, they can all be placed at the head table as long as you are comfortable with it. However, if you suspect that there are hurt feelings between the parties, you are best off placing them separately with a healthy distance in between.

SEATING ARRANGEMENTS FOR SAME SEX COUPLES

If you are two women or two men getting married, it is easy to be unclear about the seating arrangements. Tradition demands that the wedding couple sits next to the bride's mother and father—but who is the bride in this case?

In a traditional setting such as a wedding, it is nice to know that etiquette changes consistently. If you are two women getting married, you can solve it by having your fathers sit next to you; if you are two men getting married, you can have your respective mothers sit beside you.

The lady always sits to the right of her dinner companion and they usually share the first dance. The most important thing, however, is that everyone has someone they know near them. Don't be afraid to mix friends and family. Trust that your guests will find common things to talk about.

Let breastfeeding mothers sit at the ends of the tables so they can easily step away when they have to breastfeed. If the younger guests are old enough, there are many benefits to having them sit at a children's table.

⫸ Start by pairing the groups into fours. Then you can easily move them around, but still ensure that they will end up close to someone they know.

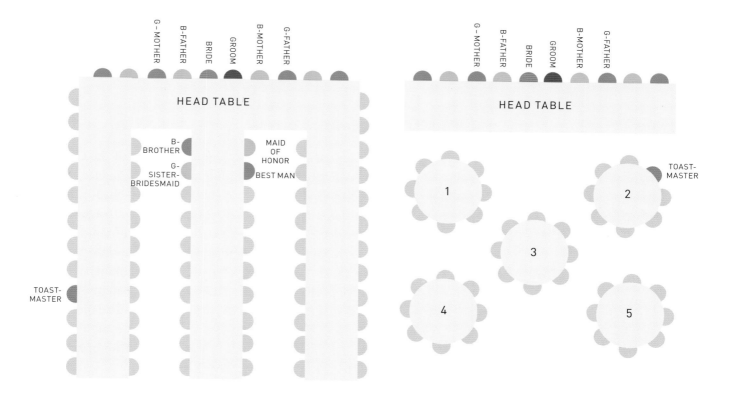

In this option,

⫸ The bride sits to the right of the groom at the middle of the head table.

⫸ The father of the bride sits to the right of the bride.

⫸ The groom's mother sits on the right of the bride's father.

⫸ The bride's mother sits on the left of the groom's father.

⫸ Bridesmaids and groomsmen often sit next to each other at the table.

⫸ The toastmaster or MC is placed where he or she can make eye contact with the wedding couple as well as the serving staff and can be heard well around the room.

⫸ The above layouts are suggestions for a family-oriented seating arrangement, but are not mandatory.

DECORATE THE RECEPTION HALL

THE RECEPTION IS A CELEBRATION you will remember for the rest of your lives. This is why you should to spend some extra time decorating the reception hall. Using detailing and various decorations, you can change the whole feel of the venue. It does not even have to cost that much. Small things such as color, shape, and flowers can make the most boring of venues into something spectacular and reshaped into a cozy or classic reception hall. Place a few candy bowls in unassuming places, decorate with pillows, and use fabric and tablecloths to add some color to the party tables.

Tables and Tablecloths

A worn out table surface can easily be hidden by a white tablecloth. If you cannot afford authentic linen, you can sew tablecloths from white sheets, which can be purchased inexpensively. Table runners in the theme color are also a nice touch. If you cannot find any table runners you like, you can use wallpaper.

Chairs

If the chairs don't match one another or are ugly, rent chair covers. These are usually white cloths decorated by a bow in your choice of color. Most often, the term "you get what you pay for" applies here—check what quality of fabric is used before renting. If you are crafty, you can create your own chair covers from sheets or buy secondhand covers.

Napkins and Napkin Rings

Linen napkins make any table setting more classy. Choose between a classic napkin fold or use napkin rings. Napkin rings come in various shapes and colors. You can either buy them as is or create your own. A nice option is to tie a silk ribbon with the theme color around the napkin.

Contact the reception hall to find out what is included in the price. Tables, chairs, glassware, flatware, and silverware are usually included, but might not look the way you want. Also research whether flower arrangements or any other décor is included in the price. If so, ask to take part in choosing colors and designs if this is important to you.

Decorations do not have to be expensive to look amazing. Beach stones, for example, are perfect alternatives to the usual seating placement cards.

⋙ Remember that
table decorations and
flowers should not be
too tall. Your guests
have to be able to see
one another!

Candleholders

An arrangement of small lanterns or a large candelabra? The kind of light source you choose will set the tone in the reception hall. Candles create a cozy atmosphere, but keep in mind that candles should not be placed directly under any flower arrangements.

Miscellaneous Fabrics for Decoration

Boring walls and ceilings can be hidden by large swathes of fabric that you can attach to the walls. Dim the lights in the areas where you want to hide discrepancies and put a spotlight on areas you want to highlight. Simple tricks to fool the eye will direct the observer to where you want them to look.

Flowers as Table Decorations

An important detail to complete the dining room is the use of flowers. Choose decorations based on what feeling you want to invoke—luxury, romance, or classic. Flower decorations can be designed in endless ways and what works best depends on what kind of table settings you have.

If you have set up long tables, it is great to place a few small arrangements at equal distances. Place single flowers—roses, for example—in candleholders or vases, in the middle of the table and at equal distances. Mix it up by placing candleholders in between every other flower; decorate the candleholders with pretty silk ribbons of the same color as the flowers for a warm impression. Another nice option is to wind ivy along the table and add some decorative touches throughout, like gold confetti.

Round tables are best with uniform arrangements on each table to give a complete look. A classic round flower bouquet in a pretty vase is a safe bet if you're not sure what to do. If you want to break the colors up, you can choose two different colors of flower arrangements—for example lilac and white—and alternate them on every other table. Another impressive solution is to fill bowls with water and float some flowers on the surface. An extra nice touch is to place a candelabra in the middle of the table and wind ivy around the base and up along the metal.

DECORATED RESTROOM

The reception hall is always decorated nicely, but many people forget the restrooms. Here are some tips for turning even the most boring restroom into a luxurious oasis.

⫸ Buy perfumed liquid soap with matching hand lotion in pretty packaging and place it next to the sink.

⫸ Put up real hand towels instead of paper ones for your guests to dry their hands.

⫸ Light scented candles for softer lighting and a pleasant aroma. Just make sure that no guests are allergic and that there are no fire hazards.

⫸ Ask someone, perhaps the maid of honor or the best man, to make sure the restrooms are in good condition throughout the evening and that there is always toilet paper available.

⫸ Arrange a beautiful basket or box with emergency items that you and your guests might need throughout the evening.

Table Decorations

There are a few things to keep in mind when decorating the tables.

- Tall table decorations can obstruct everyone's view and will make it difficult for guests to communicate with one another across the table.

- Decorations, such as small stones or acrylic diamonds, can be nice touches for the tables but are difficult to clean up if they fall on the floor. Instead, place them at the bottom of vases as a beautiful touch.

- Choose inexpensive flowers in your theme colors to reduce the cost of the table decorations.

- Bring the flowers you used to decorate the church and use them as table decorations to save money.

- Have vases ready on the tables for the bridal and bridesmaids' bouquets to prevent them from wilting before the night is over. They are also perfect as additional decorations for the head table.

- Find out what kind of flowers are most durable so you can decorate the reception hall the night before. Certain flowers, such as lilacs, wilt quickly and are not well suited for table arrangements.

AN UNERRING THEME

- Have you chosen a specific theme for your wedding? Let it show! If you have, for example, chosen a movie theme, tie this into the table settings by naming the tables after movies or actors, place popcorn bowls and Oscar statues on tables, and roll out the red carpet. Dare to be extravagant and give the guests a theme party they will never forget!

HOW YOUR TOASTMASTER
CAN SUCCEED

It is true that it is an honor to be chosen as the toastmaster or Master of Ceremonies, but you should be sure to choose the right person for the job. The toastmaster or MC will be taking care of a great many things during your day and it is a very important job, so choose the person with great care. Some couples prefer to ask a close friend to serve as toastmaster or MC, while others choose to hire a professional. It is the toastmaster's duties to keep the list of the speeches and the schedule, to present the speakers during the dinner, and to arrange any funny games and pranks. Sometimes, the toastmaster or MC is in charge of the whole reception, in which case, the wedding planner may be a good person to fill this role.

It is important for you to sit down and talk with your toastmaster or MC to relay your expectations for the reception and make sure you are on the same page regarding his or her role. Sometimes, the toastmaster's role is only to introduce the speakers during the dinner and in other cases, he or she is the director of the whole reception. This can entail assignments such as arranging the rice tossing outside the church, going shopping for gag gifts, and making sure that the reception hall has everything you need. This can be especially important if you do not have a host couple handling these tasks.

Make sure the toastmaster or MC coordinates with the kitchen so that everyone has a schedule to keep track of time. The speeches should be scheduled in between the dishes to keep the guests from having to eat cold food.

KEEP TRACK OF THE SPEECHES

≫ It is the MC or toastmaster's duty to keep track of who is supposed to speak and when. He or she should have already spoken to those who are planning to speak about the sequence and volume. If there are many people who want to speak, it is a good idea to set a time limit on the speeches—otherwise you'll end up with too much of a good thing.

DON'T FORGET THE LOVE!

≫ It is important that the toastmaster or MC doesn't forget to celebrate the love between the bride and groom. After all, that is why everyone is there. He or she can toast the couple and their love for one another in a lovely and surprising manner. For example, the toastmaster can film the couple's closest family and friends sharing their thoughts about the couple's relationship. The film can be accompanied by touching music and pictures of the couple and can be shown during dinner. Or, the toastmaster can plan a surprise performance in which a guest sings the couple's favorite song.

During the Reception Dinner

It is during the actual dinner that the toastmaster or Master of Ceremonies has the most responsibilities and should therefore be sure not to drink too much alcohol, even though he or she should have fun. The toastmaster or MC has a lot of duties—here are some of the most important ones:

1.

Your toastmaster shows all guests where the seating charts are so they can find their way to their seats.

2.

The toastmaster or MC introduces him or herself when everyone has been seated and reviews the practical information, such as location of restrooms and when there will be breaks in the schedule for people to stretch their legs.

3.

The toastmaster or MC is free to introduce each speaker by giving the audience some background about how they know the couple. The toast-master can also offer a funny anecdote to warm up the guests. Since the toastmaster has to make him or herself heard, it might be a good idea to give him or her a bell to ring to get the attention of the guests.

4.

It is the duty of the toastmaster or MC to make sure that nothing happens that is not supposed to. For example, the toastmaster shouldn't let Uncle George stand up and make a toast beginning "Congratulations Martin and Christina" when it's actually Martin and Lydia who are getting married.

5.

The toastmaster or MC should clearly inform the speakers well ahead of time to let them know what timeframe they need to stay within. Three to four minutes per speech is usually the norm. If a speaker is starting to ramble, it's the toastmaster's duty to make the person end his or her speech by making eye contact and looking at the clock.

For the
Safe Journey Home
of your napkin ring

Helene & Henrik

TIPS FOR A MEMORABLE NIGHT

≫ Arrange a trivia quiz about the couple. Include questions such as: When did the couple meet? Where did they have their first kiss? Perhaps the grand prize can be a nice dinner with the couple.

≫ Place a typewriter in the reception hall and let your guests type personal messages and well wishes on it.

≫ Create a wedding tree! Carefully draw a tree trunk with branches on a sturdy piece of paper. Place it in the reception hall along with a small jar of green finger paint. Then let your guests dip their fingers in the paint and make a thumbprint on the tree to create a tree full of leaves. Frame the tree and hang it on the wall as a happy memory.

≫ Create a Spotify list where each guest can put his or her favorite love song on it. It will be a lovely memory and something for you to listen to on all your wedding anniversaries.

≫ Placing goodie bags at each seat is usually much appreciated. Fill it with candy or write a personal greeting to each guest.

SPEECHES

FEW MOMENTS ARE as intimately associated with speech as weddings are, but unfortunately this often means that the speeches will run too long and there will be too many of them. According to tradition, the couple does not have to make a speech in front of friends and family, but rather the father of the bride and the and father of the groom do. This is however a tradition worth breaking. Be inspired by romantic declarations of love and melt your partner's heart!

First up is the bridal toast. A bridal toast is not a speech, but rather a toast to the wedding couple. It begins the festivities and can be done by the host couple, the best man, or the maid of honor. It is a short and sweet toast along the lines of "We wish the newly married couple the best of luck and prosperity. Cheers to the happy couple!" The bridal toast is only one toast and can be held before dinner with a heartfelt hurrah at the end.

The host couple or the toastmaster or Master of Ceremonies are often the first speakers to welcome the guests when they are seated at the table and have gotten something to drink. This welcome speech, as well as all the other speeches, should be kept short. It is then time for the tearful speech traditionally given by the bride's father. This speech is usually personal, moving, and funny, but should not last longer than three minutes. If the father of the bride is not in attendance, the mother of the bride can give a speech instead.

After this, it is time for the groom's father, who gives an equally clever and touching speech. If you are traditionalists, the next speaker should be the person who conducted your ceremony—this is, however, not that common anymore. Usually, this is followed by one of the older relatives of either groom or bride, which is always appreciated by the guests. At this point, you have already had five speeches, and this is before the best man and maid of honor get to speak, not to mention siblings, friends, neighbors, and any others who wish to say a few words.

The toastmaster or MC clearly has a serious job ahead of him or her to make sure that all the guests have a chance to enjoy the food and conversation and are not just listening to speeches. It is often a big challenge to make sure the speeches are varied and are kept short. Songs, poems, and other funny acts are usually appreciated in between traditional speeches. Spontaneous speeches by guests who have had a bit too much to drink are just embarrassing and should be deterred by the toastmaster. Guests who want to hold a speech or do a funny act should contact the toastmaster or MC—not the wedding couple.

TIPS FOR THE NERVOUS SPEAKER

≫ Use a cheat sheet, if for no other reason than to have something to do with your hands.

≫ Keep your eyes on the bride and pretend it is just you and her. If you want to turn toward the guests, place your eyes right above their heads and avoid eye contact.

≫ Be personable, but avoid embarrassing memories.

≫ Practice your speech in advance and time it.

≫ Mistakes that break the ice are sometimes used as a rhetorical measure. Silence offers some time for reflection.

≫ For anyone who feels unsure of their talents in writing a speech, there are plenty of speeches to be found on the Internet.

BUFFET OR
THREE-COURSE MEAL?

MOST COUPLES OFFER something to eat at their reception. A nice dinner with speeches is a big part of the event and it gives people a chance to get to know each another. But it can be difficult to know how to go about this. Perhaps you have considered having a buffet instead of a three-course meal. Keep in mind that every reception hall has different rules and regulations and bringing outside food and drink is not always allowed.

Classic Seated Three-Course Dinner

The most common meal at the reception is still the seated three-course dinner consisting of an appetizer, main course, and dessert. Talk about your wishes with the chef well in advance to create a balanced menu and keep in mind seasonal ingredients that are often cheaper and tastier. Also remember that not all dishes are suited to make in large quantities.

At a traditional three-course dinner, guests are seated at tables during the whole meal and the dishes are served by serving staff. Be sure to have enough staff to serve the whole party at the same time; otherwise guests may have to wait for their food, which puts a considerable damper on the festivities. The toastmaster or MC should make sure that the guests get their main course at least fifteen minutes before the speeches begin. This is just to ensure that the food won't get cold. Also, make sure to mark down any special allergies or food requirements on the seating chart for the staff.

A smart way to handle logistics it to have the appetizer already on the tables when the party is seated. Just be sure to choose ingredients that are not heat sensitive if you are getting married in the summertime.

Choose dishes that are suitable for serving in large quantities and won't get cold if they are meant to be served hot.

Buffet

By setting up a few dishes on a long table, you create a buffet for guests to serve themselves. The benefit of this is that guests can choose what they like, but the downside is that there will be more commotion during the dinner.

If you are planning on cooking your own food, you should prepare as much as you can in the weeks before the wedding and then freeze the food for the reception. It can be difficult to figure out what dishes will be most popular, so it's best to cook more than you think you will need. Place the dishes on each side of the table so guests can serve themselves from both sides. Complete the buffet with bread and pasta, which are very filling. It should be clear to everyone what dishes are intended for vegetarians and people with allergies. Make sure to have plenty of extras, just in case other guests try some of these dishes.

Have the serving staff refill the buffet as the dinner moves along to make sure there is enough for everyone. It's not fun for the last guests if they're left with only scraps.

⫸ At a buffet, it is easy to choose your menu based on your theme. Offer a barbeque buffet at an outdoor reception or seafood at a beach reception.

⫸ Have one table at a time go up to the buffet to avoid crowding. Be sure to refill the trays in between servings.

Mingling with Canapés

If you don't want a big reception that goes late into the night, you can choose to hold a mingling session following the ceremony. Offer some canapés and snacks with champagne while you socialize with your guests. A tea party served with delicious mini pastries can also be a nice alternative if you want your day to be alcohol free.

Clearly state on your invitation what will be served so your guests know. Some guests may not have had lunch before the mingling session, so let them take a little bit more. Make sure you have enough for everyone. Also, let people know when the mingling is over to avoid any misunderstandings.

If you want to keep costs down, but still want to serve champagne, you can offer real champagne for the bridal toast and then a simple sparkling wine for dinner.

DRINKS

>>> A bridal toast is a simple aperitif—champagne, punch, or sparkling cider—that the guests will drink when the wedding couple arrives at the reception hall. It can be held outside or at the tables but most often it takes place during mingling.

TAKE SOME EXTRA time to consider what drinks to serve at dinner. The right drink can enhance any meal, and for best results you should plan both food and drink at the same time. Even the most luxurious of wines can fall short if it they are served with the wrong dish, and a wine of lesser quality can ruin a great dinner.

The drink budget will obviously be affected by whether the reception hall or the restaurant will supply alcohol or if you will be bringing your own. If you have the opportunity to bring it yourselves, there are many opportunities to obtain great wines at a decent price.

It is not easy to offer general advice for pairing drinks with red meat and seafood. Ask the staff at the liquor store; they can usually offer the best advice on drinks that complement your menu and work within your budget. Keep in mind that sometimes the liquor store might have to special order your requests, so make sure to do this well ahead of time. If you choose to serve boxed wine, pour the wine into nice-looking decanters. Also make sure all guests have water glasses at their tables.

For an aperitif, sparkling wine is the most common choice. If you have a limited budget, Cava makes a great alternative to champagne. If you prefer, you can always serve a drink during mingling as well. It is a nice touch to choose a seasonal beverage; for example, offer something warm at a winter wedding and a cool, refreshing drink at a summer wedding.

If you have a chosen a theme for the wedding, this can also be reflected in your drink choice. If you have a French theme, you can show this by serving French wines, or if you are passionate about the environment, you can serve organic wine.

It can be difficult to calculate the volume of alcohol you will need—some people drink more than others. A good rule of thumb is that you will always use more if the bottles are on the tables than if the staff serves the guests. Usually, you serve one glass of wine for the appetizer and two glasses for the main course. In addition, you might want to serve an after-dinner drink or dessert wine.

If the dinner is followed by entertainment, you should consider what kind of bar you want to have. It's not easy to calculate how much liquor you will need for the reception and the amount will vary depending on how long the party lasts and if it is hot inside the reception hall. It is better to buy too much than too little, and some stores may allow you to return unopened bottles.

If the guests will be asked to pay for drinks, this should be clearly stated on the invitations. Also state if there is a discount or if the guests will have to pay full price for the drinks.

To Serve Alcohol or Not?

Alcohol can be a sensitive question for some people. If there is someone in the family who cannot handle their liquor, you may not be tempted to invite him or her to your wedding. But there are a few tricks to limit their intake.

- Opt for a non-alcoholic wedding.

- The earlier you hold your wedding, the less alcohol you are expected to serve. Get married early in the day and celebrate with a lunch.

- Serve non-alcoholic sparkling cider as a welcome toast. This is appreciated by those guests who will be the designated drivers.

- Placing water on all the tables will keep the guests from drinking as much alcohol. Swap the after-dinner drink for a non-alcoholic alternative, like a chocolate drink in a shot glass. This will be perceived as a cute idea rather than a cheap one.

- Hand out drink tickets to all guests, and once they have been used, start charging for all drinks. Or have guests pay for their drinks throughout the reception—this is usually a great way to curb any excessive drinking.

If you hire a catering company, it's a good idea to ask for a signed contract where it clearly states how much alcohol is included and what kind of alcohol it is. Ask for several quotes from various vendors to find a company that suits you both in price and offerings.

BUDGETING TIP

Do you want to offer champagne but worry that it might get too expensive? Opt for real champagne for the bridal toast and then offer sparkling wine after that.

Boxed wine is perhaps most economical, but make sure to pour the wine into lovely decanters to make it look nicer. The wine will actually taste better as well.

THE WEDDING CAKE

MOST COUPLES choose to serve cake after the reception dinner. The wedding couple usually cuts the first piece of cake together and they eat it in front of the guests, who are served cake after this. If the reception is held at a restaurant, the staff will usually cut the cake for the guests. It is also common for the cake to be included in the package the restaurant offers, so check what applies to your venue.

Some restaurants do not want to make wedding cakes, because it is such a demanding task, and you will have to bring your own cake to the venue. Please do not try to make your own wedding cake! It is both time-consuming and expensive! Order a cake from a bakery and have them deliver it.

Dessert and Cake?

If you have chosen a wedding menu with several courses it can feel like a bit too much to serve dessert after the meal. Instead, choose a light dessert such as a mousse with fruit or berries. If you worry that there will just be too much, you can always omit dessert and instead serve the cake after dinner. Another alternative is to serve dessert before the first dance and the cake after it to let the dinner digest. Another, quite unconventional option is to cut the cake at the bridal toast. This is when the guests are getting hungry and will probably appreciate the cake the most.

Marzipan or Fondant

At local bakeries, wedding cakes are often very traditional in appearance and are covered in white marzipan and decorated by marzipan flowers. But recently, many stores now offer wedding cakes where the wedding couple can request various imaginative designs. The cakes can look any way you like, and you can even incorporate your theme onto them.

Sometimes weddings cakes are covered in frosting, but fondant is more common. Fondant looks like marzipan but is smoother, sweeter, and is perfect for people with nut allergies.

⫸ Are you unsure of what cake to order? Ask for a consultation at a bakery. This way, you will have the opportunity to review your options and sample different flavor combinations. In certain cases, the bakery charges a consultation fee, which is usually deducted from your final bill.

⫸ If you have ordered an extravagant and expensive cake, you should ask for a signed contract. This will assure that you get what you pay for.

⫸ If the design of the cake is important to you, ask to see pictures of other cakes the bakery has made so you can get an idea of what yours will look like. If you want a tiered cake, it is important to choose a baker who has experience with this.

⫸ It takes more time than you might think to make a wedding cake, so make doubly sure you really want to do it on your own.

⫸ Before you book your reception hall, you should ask if the cake is included in the menu. It is not always included due to health codes. If you are not satisfied with the options they offer, you should resolve this before booking the venue.

⫸ Order your cake well in advance. This is especially important if you have chosen a small company and a special design. Naturally, you should also offer a tasty alternative for guests with food restrictions.

The fondant can be in any color you like, but bright white fondant is especially perfect for weddings.

Decorate the cake with edible flowers or any other decorations. Even if it's still common to place figurines on top of the cake, it is not a requirement. Some people place a mini version of the bouquet on top of the cake.

Tiered Cake

If you are planning a big wedding with many guests, you will probably need more than one cake. The most common thing to do is to order several of the same cake in varying sizes and then have them placed on top of each other in tiers. This is easy to transport and serve.

If you want a tiered cake where the cakes are stacked directly on top of each other, it is important to ask your baker if this can be done. A certain technique is required to do this to secure the bottom tiers and not every baker is able to do it. There are certain fillings that are better suited for this; they have to be firmer in consistency to maintain the shape of the cake. A tiered cake also complicates the transportation, since it is sensitive to bumps and sharp turns in the road. If you still want a tiered cake, it can be worth paying a delivery fee to have it delivered to you.

Other Options

There are other options if you don't want a traditional wedding cake. For the last few years it has become more and more common to offer cupcakes or mini cakes. These allow you to offer several flavors and also alternatives for allergy sufferers. Another hot trend right now is to have a candy or dessert table. It is definitely a delight to look at several desserts of all the colors of the rainbow. And if you still want to cut a cake, you can order a small one in addition to the desserts.

There are many fun figurines you can decorate the cake with. You can even order a cake with your own faces on the marzipan.

DANCING WITH EASE

WHERE THERE IS A WEDDING, there is a first dance. If you are not comfortable in the spotlight, it can be stressful to have to dance the first dance in front of all the guests, but there are some tricks for easing the pressure on couples with two left feet. According to tradition, the wedding couple begins the dance alone on the dance floor and after a little while other close relatives follow suit. One suggestion is to ask your parents and other relatives to join you early in the dance, which will make the rest of the party join you on the dance floor.

There is really no specific dance called the bridal or wedding dance, but it's usually a waltz—just remember that you don't necessarily have to waltz to it. It is always entertaining if the wedding couple surprises the guests with a rehearsed number, no matter what kind of dance it is. Remember that it is your day and you get to decide! If you want your dance to be perfect, you can always take a few lessons before the wedding.

Music for the Reception

Weddings are about happiness, and what's better than music and dancing? How well you have planned the musical entertainment will determine the success of the reception. Music has always been linked to weddings, and, in earlier times, musicians used to play on the way to the church as well as from the church to the reception hall. These days, it is common to hire a DJ or to even ask some musically-inclined friends to handle the entertainment. Arrange for this well in advance and ask yourselves what suits you best. Here are some suggestions at various price points.

ALMOST FREE: YOUR OWN PLAYLIST. If you own an mp3 player, the musical component can be completely free of cost. Create a playlist with your favorite songs and then plug your mp3 player into some speakers. Another option is to use Spotify's pay services (otherwise you will end up with commercial breaks—a total killjoy).

BUDGET: ELECTRONIC DJ. There are several options if you want to rent equipment with music included in the package price. You can, for example, rent automatic music equipment, where you mix the songs you have chosen in advance through the company website. You will then get all the technical equipment, like speakers, included. Another option is to rent a mixing table, speakers, and cords to plug in your mp3 player or computer.

MID-RANGE. A live DJ who chooses the music and plays albums is another option. An established DJ has most likely played at weddings before and knows what works and is appreciated and can therefore adjust the music according to taste and requests. It feels a little bit more fancy than just having a digital playlist. It can be a little complicated to find the right DJ, so ask for recommendations.

LUXURY. A live band will have the guests dancing their shoes off and will make a life-long memory. There are various live bands to choose from—anything from cover bands to jazz bands. Look for bands with experience doing weddings. Ask yourselves whether you want a certain genre of music and then compare different bands (some have samples available for you on their home pages). The price will vary depending on the experience of the band and their equipment, among other things.

⋙ Choose music that most people will enjoy.

8 Rules of Etiquette for Guests!

WHERE DO I PUT MY PURSE DURING DINNER?

It is best to keep a large bag under your chair. A small evening bag can stay in your lap. If you choose to hang it on your chair, make sure it does not obstruct the serving staff in their duties.

CAN I BLOW MY NOSE DURING DINNER IF I HAVE A COLD?

Blowing your nose close to food is not proper etiquette. Excuse yourself and walk outside to do what you have to do away from everyone else.

CAN I KEEP MY CELL PHONE ON SILENT MODE DURING DINNER?

You should not have your phone on at all or even with you during dinner. Talking on the phone during dinner is very rude. If you expect an important phone call from the babysitter, you can leave the cell phone with a staff member and ask them to take the call for you.

WHEN CAN I TAKE OFF MY SUIT JACKET?

The answer is really never. But if the groom or the host takes off his jacket you can follow suit to make their blunder less obvious.

WHEN CAN I START EATING?

After the hostess has begun eating or said "enjoy your meal." When it comes to similar questions, there are certain golden rules and it is always a good idea to wait until the hostess or the wedding couple has begun before you start.

WHEN IS IT OKAY FOR ME TO GO OUT TO SMOKE?

It does not matter how badly you want a cigarette. You should not take any initiative when it comes to smoking. Wait until the toastmaster or Master of Ceremonies gives the green light for this.

CAN I GET SECOND HELPINGS IF IT IS A BUFFET?

If you know that you are going to be hungry, you would do best to ask the host couple about any limitations to the buffet.

CAN I EAT OR DRINK DURING SPEECHES?

No, you should not. Remember that the people who have plucked up the courage to speak deserve your full attention.

The ABCs of Weddings

BACHELOR PARTY

Going back to the 1700s, the friends of the groom filled him with liquor before they brought him to his intended wife. The modern bachelor party was created by the bourgeois circles in the mid-1800s and since then, it has developed into one of the most easygoing customs we have today.

BANNS OF MARRIAGE

The banns of marriage were a public announcement that two people intended to marry. The purpose for this was to bring to attention any legal impediments why the intended couple could not be married. The banns date back to 1216 and were abolished in the Roman Catholic Church in 1873.

BACHELORETTE PARTY

A party for the bride, arranged by the bride's friends. What started off as an innocent event has now evolved into today's playful party. The party is usually held a day or two before the wedding. Some consider bachelorette parties to be inappropriate, while others think it's a great opportunity to celebrate their friendship. Some get dressed up to perform in a public place by singing and selling kisses, others bar-hop, and many have a lovely day together at a spa and end it with a nice dinner.

BEST MAN

This best man's duties vary between countries. It is usually the groom's best friend or brother who is asked to be best man. According to tradition, the best man is dressed just like the groom and both of them wait at the front of the altar for the bride and her father.

BETROTHAL

In the past, the betrothal was a legally-binding agreement between bride and groom. In 1571, the church stated: "Betrothal with gifts, in front of witnesses, with consummation to follow, is declared binding and right in front of God." The betrothal was binding without a wedding ceremony in the church and allowed for sexual relations, and any potential children were allowed to inherit. The agreement was confirmed by a handshake and thereby the term: "To give one's hand."

BOUTONNIÈRE

A boutonnière is a flower for the buttonhole in the left suit lapel. The groom wears a boutonnière during the wedding ceremony.

BRIDAL BOUQUET

A bridal bouquet is the bouquet the bride holds in her hands at the wedding ceremony. One tradition dictates that after the ceremony, the bride tosses her bouquet over her shoulder to the unmarried female guests. The one who catches it will be the next one to get married. However, most of today's brides save their bouquets.

CAKE

The traditional wedding cake has several tiers and is decorated by a wedding couple figurine on top. Today, there are many variations and it is even common to send the guests home with a slice of cake, since many will be too full to eat cake after a big dinner.

DANCE

The wedding couple shares the first dance, which usually is a waltz. Soon afterward, the rest of the bridal party joins in. Etiquette demands that each gentleman dances with the lady he is seated with at the table. After that, he dances with his wife or girlfriend and then with the lady across the table.

DIVORCED PARENTS

It is your day and you have the right to have all your parents attending, no matter if they are divorced or remarried. If you are worried about it being uncomfortable, you can always seat the divorced couples at opposite sides of the room.

DOWRY

This used to be a gift from the parents to their children when they were ready to make their own homes. Lately, it has come to signify the wealth the bride brings with her to the new home.

ENGAGEMENT

With the development of bourgeois culture, exchanging rings became a sign of betrothal, but they did not promise any rights to consummation and were not legally binding agreements. The engagement today is the first romantic step to officially proclaiming your status as a couple. The engagement is an introduction of one's intended life partner without any legal meaning; it simply means that you have promised to marry. According to custom, the wedding should take place within a year of exchanging rings.

FLOWER GIRL AND RING BEARER

Children who walk ahead of the wedding couple to and from the altar. The boy is designated as ring bearer and the girl is a flower girl.

GROOMSMAN

A groomsman is a functionary during the official event. At the wedding, it is common for the groomsmen to guide the guests to their seats in church, to help them with their coats, and to arrange for transportation at the wedding ceremony and the reception if they don't have their own cars.

HONEYMOON

The honeymoon is a trip following the wedding that lasts for a week or two. It is an important time for the couple to get used to their new titles of man and wife and to rest up after all the wedding preparations.

HOPE CHEST

In the olden days, brides used to collect linen and kitchenware in their hope chests to prepare for married life. This tradition has existed since the Middle Ages and still exists in certain places today. These chests have always been richly decorated and artfully painted. The chest contains various linens you would need for a new home—towels, sheets, tablecloths, napkins, and clothes.

HOST COUPLE

The host couple helps out with all the things that have to be taken care of surrounding the wedding, everything from managing the guest list and wedding presents to taking care of the guests on the actual wedding day. If the parents have paid for the wedding, they usually take on the hosting duties for the wedding.

INTERCESSOR

The intercessor used to be the person who represented the man proposing to the girl's father. It was his duty to sell the father on all the great attributes of the intended groom so the father would consent to the marriage.

INVITATIONS

You should send out your wedding invitations no later than a month before the wedding, but it is best to send them out much earlier than that. The invitations should clearly state the time, place, dress code, how to RSVP, and whether the invitation is both to the wedding ceremony and reception or just to the reception.

LAST NAME

On the marriage license application, you will fill out which last name you choose; you will have the opportunity to keep your name or to just add your partner's last name. If you do not apply for a new last name, you will automatically keep your individual last names, but you still have the option to change your name at later date.

MAID OF HONOR

A maid of honor was once a virgin who attended the queen. Today, a maid of honor is often a sister or a friend of the bride. It is her duty to hold the bridal bouquet during the wedding ceremony and to straighten out the train and veil. Often the maid of honor will hold a smaller bouquet. She is formally dressed, but should not wear white.

MARRIAGE

Marriage is what you enter into when you say "I do." It is not only a testimony of your love for one another, but also the beginning of a wonderful life together, which will go through ups and downs. Nurture your love with care and kindness.

MARRIAGE LICENSE

A marriage license is a document issued by a governmental authority that allows two people to get married. A marriage license is valid for only a specific time period, usually from 30 to 90 days, depending on the state.

PROPOSAL

It used to be the man's privilege to propose, except on leap year when women were allowed to make a proposal. These days, anyone can propose to whomever they like—man or woman.

RICE

After the wedding ceremony, the tradition is to throw rice on the newly wedded couple. It is an old fertility ritual that promises to bring the house and home many riches. Since birds may eat the rice (which is dangerous for them), you should sweep it up after you are done. You can also toss rose petals, or confetti, or blow soap bubbles.

RING

The jewelry on your left hand is the only thing that visually declares you are married. At a civil wedding, you don't need rings, but at most church weddings, you are required to exchange them. Most people still choose to exchange rings as a proclamation of their love.

SECOND OR THIRD MARRIAGES

It is becoming more and more common that one or both parties has been married before. Even though our society offers more equality today, it is still normal for the bride to tone down her second wedding, and some people do not approve of women wearing veils or white dresses for their second wedding. Don't pay attention to what other people think! If you love each other, your wedding should be just the way you want it.

SPEECHES

Speeches are intimately associated with weddings. The speech given by the bride's father used to be the most important one, but these days anyone can give a speech and it is the duty of the toastmaster or the Master of Ceremonies to keep track of them.

TELEGRAM

For a long time, the telegram has been the standard way to send well wishes when a guest cannot attend the wedding. Usually the toastmaster or the Master of Ceremonies reads the telegrams when coffee is being served.

THANK YOU CARD

It is customary for the wedding couple to send out thank you cards, often paired with a wedding photo, to all their guests to thank them for attending.

TOASTMASTER OR TOASTMADAME

The person appointed to announce speakers, hold toasts, and read telegrams during the wedding dinner. This function may also be performed by the Master of Ceremonies.

TRANSPORTATION

The wedding couple rides in the front to the reception hall. For this occasion, many rent or borrow a vehicle—perhaps an old car or horse and buggy. Choose your vehicle based on the type of wedding you are having, perhaps a Rolls Royce if you have your wedding at a castle or something similar. Going from church to the small country farm, a Chevrolet might be more suitable, or a horse and buggy.

WEDDING

The word *wedding* comes from the Old English word "weddung," or "weddian to pledge."

WEDDING CEREMONY

The wedding ceremony is the ritual that symbolizes the entry into marriage.

WEDDING GIFT

It is a tradition for the groom to give the bride a wedding gift the day after the wedding. It is common today for both bride and groom to give one another gifts the day after the wedding.

WEDDING MARCH

The wedding march is the music that plays when the wedding couple walks in and out of the church. In earlier times, the wedding march was played by musicians following the bridal party to the church and the wedding party.

WEDDING OFFICIATOR

The wedding officiator is the person who has the legal authority to perform the matrimonial ceremony. For a wedding ceremony to be legal, it has to be conducted by an authorized officiator. This can be a priest, minister, or rabbi or a civil servant.

WEDDING VOWS

The vows are a part of the wedding ceremony, and they often read: "I take you to be my lawfully wedded wife/husband, to have and to hold, in sickness and in health, until death do us part." You can also write your own vows.

CHECKLIST

Planning a wedding takes time, and there are a lot of things to think about and research. Is the church available on your date? Perhaps you want to get married on a cliff by the sea and need to find a wedding officiator? Have you found the right reception hall? Where will all the guests stay? And don't forget about cake! Count down to your wedding with a checklist.

ABOUT A YEAR IN ADVANCE

◯ Visit trade shows for a head start

◯ Create a budget

◯ Open a wedding bank account

◯ Book a potential wedding planner

◯ Book the wedding venue

◯ Book the wedding officiator

◯ Book the reception hall

◯ Book the photographer

◯ Assign a host couple, toastmaster, maid of honor, and best man

◯ Create a guest list

◯ Mail save-the-date cards

ABOUT SIX MONTHS IN ADVANCE

◯ Decide on a theme

◯ Design invitations and other print items

◯ Book a potential catering firm

◯ Book entertainment for ceremony and reception

◯ Sew, buy, or rent all wedding attire

◯ Book a hairdresser and makeup artist

◯ Choose wedding cake and baker

◯ Book the honeymoon

◯ Research potential visas and vaccinations

ABOUT THREE MONTHS IN ADVANCE

- ◯ Send out invitations
- ◯ Buy wedding bands and order inscriptions
- ◯ Book a honeymoon suite
- ◯ Book transportation from ceremony to reception
- ◯ Order flowers
- ◯ Send in applications for a marriage license
- ◯ Make a gift registry
- ◯ Buy underwear, shoes, accessories, and jewelry
- ◯ Practice the first dance
- ◯ Talk about your wishes with your entertainers
- ◯ Write a potential prenuptial agreement with an attorney
- ◯ Meet with the wedding officiator and run through the ceremony

....
....
....

A MONTH IN ADVANCE

- ◯ Finalize seating arrangements
- ◯ Double check that your passports are valid
- ◯ Consult with your hairdresser and makeup artist
- ◯ Taste test your menu
- ◯ Try on all clothes and see if you need any alterations made
- ◯ Meet with the photographer and decide on details
- ◯ Drop off the wedding bands for polishing
- ◯ Prepare the schedule for the wedding day with everyone involved
- ◯ Double-check all bookings
- ◯ Create wedding programs, reception programs, menus, and placecards
- ◯ Arrange for table decorations
- ◯ Buy wedding gifts
- ◯ Buy gifts for the bridal party
- ◯ Buy a guest book and a pen
- ◯ Walk in your shoes

....
....
....

A WEEK BEFORE THE WEDDING

- ◯ Confirm final head count with reception hall
- ◯ Print the seating chart
- ◯ Pick up wedding bands
- ◯ Double check transportation schedule
- ◯ Rehearse the wedding ceremony and submit the marriage license to the officiator
- ◯ Prepare an emergency bag with scissors, band-aids, and other necessary items
- ◯ Try on attire one last time
- ◯ Pack bags for the wedding night and honeymoon
- ◯ Get a manicure

....
....

THE DAY BEFORE

- ◯ Decorate the reception hall
- ◯ Relax and go to bed early

....
....

THE BIG DAY

- ◯ Head to the hairdresser
- ◯ Arrange for flower and cake pick up
- ◯ Say "I do!"

....
....

WITHIN SIX MONTHS AFTER THE WEDDING

- ◯ Write thank you cards
- ◯ Develop photos
- ◯ Relax and enjoy your honeymoon!

....
....
....
....
....

BUDGET LIST

To ease your planning, you can use a budget list. Here is a list of the most
common items that are included in a wedding. Fill out your anticipated costs,
and as you go along fill out the actual costs.

	VENDOR	BUDGET	ACTUAL COST
BRIDE			
Dress			
Petticoat			
Veil			
Tiara/hair decorations			
Wedding band			
Miscellaneous jewelry			
Shoes			
Underwear			
Pantyhose			
Garter			
Evening bag			
Shawl/coat			
Hairdresser			
Makeup			
Manicure			
TOTAL:			

	VENDOR	BUDGET	ACTUAL COST
BRIDAL PARTY			
Dress for maid of honor			
Attire for best man			
Styling			
Potential gifts			
TOTAL:			

	VENDOR	BUDGET	ACTUAL COST

GROOM

Suit/Tuxedo			
Shirt			
Tie/bowtie/handkerchief/cummerbund			
Vest			
Suspenders			
Wedding band			
Shoes			
Underwear			
Cufflinks			
TOTAL:			

PRINTED ITEMS

Save-the-date cards			
Invitations			
Wedding program			
Menu			
Reception program			
Placecards			
Guest book			
Thank you cards			
Stamps			
TOTAL:			

	VENDOR	BUDGET	ACTUAL COST

WEDDING CEREMONY

	VENDOR	BUDGET	ACTUAL COST
Venue/wedding officiator			
Soloist			
Musicians			
Decorations			
Transportation for wedding couple			
Transportation for guests			
Rice /flower petals			
Coffee/pastries			
TOTAL:			

RECEPTION

	VENDOR	BUDGET	ACTUAL COST
Venue			
Food			
Drink			
Cake			
Snacks			
Tables/chairs			
Silverware/glassware/ flatware			
Tablecloths/napkins			
Napkin rings			
Miscellaneous decorations			
Serving staff			
Entertainment			
Dance lessons			
Cleaning			
TOTAL:			

	VENDOR	BUDGET	ACTUAL COST

FLOWERS

Bridal bouquet			
Boutonnière			
Wedding decorations			
Table decorations			
Flower archway			
TOTAL:			

PHOTOGRAPHY

Photographer			
Videographer			
Albums			
Thank you cards			
Announcement in local paper			
TOTAL:			

OTHER

Wedding coordinator			
Wedding night			
Taxi			
Wedding gifts			
Honeymoon			
TOTAL:			

GRAND TOTAL:	VENDOR	BUDGET	ACTUAL COST

GUEST LIST

		Attending	Not attending

Name .... Number of guests .... ○ ○

Notes ....

Name .... Number of guests .... ○ ○

Notes ....

Name .... Number of guests .... ○ ○

Notes ....

Name .... Number of guests .... ○ ○

Notes ....

Name .... Number of guests .... ○ ○

Notes ....

Name .... Number of guests .... ○ ○

Notes ....

Name .... Number of guests .... ○ ○

Notes ....

Name .... Number of guests .... ○ ○

Notes ....

Name .... Number of guests .... ○ ○

Notes ....

Name .... Number of guests .... ○ ○

Notes ....

Name .... Number of guests .... ○ ○

Notes ....

Name .... Number of guests .... ○ ○

Notes ....

Name .... Number of guests .... ○ ○

Notes ....

		Attending	Not attending

Name .... Number of guests .... ○ ○

Notes ....

Name .... Number of guests .... ○ ○

Notes ....

Name .... Number of guests .... ○ ○

Notes ....

Name .... Number of guests .... ○ ○

Notes ....

Name .... Number of guests .... ○ ○

Notes ....

Name .... Number of guests .... ○ ○

Notes ....

Name .... Number of guests .... ○ ○

Notes ....

Name .... Number of guests .... ○ ○

Notes ....

Name .... Number of guests .... ○ ○

Notes ....

Name .... Number of guests .... ○ ○

Notes ....

Name .... Number of guests .... ○ ○

Notes ....

Name .... Number of guests .... ○ ○

Notes ....

Name .... Number of guests .... ○ ○

Notes ....

Name .... Number of guests .... ○ ○

Notes ....

Name .... Number of guests .... ○ ○

Notes ....

Name .... Number of guests .... ○ ○

Notes ....

Name .... Number of guests .... ○ ○

Notes ....

Name .... Number of guests .... ○ ○

Notes ....

Name .... Number of guests .... ○ ○

Notes ....

Name .... Number of guests .... ○ ○

Notes ....

Name .... Number of guests .... ○ ○

Notes ....

Name .... Number of guests .... ○ ○

Notes ....

Name .... Number of guests .... ○ ○

Notes ....

Name .... Number of guests .... ○ ○

Notes ....

Name .... Number of guests .... ○ ○

Notes ....

Name .... Number of guests .... ○ ○

Notes ....

RSVP date ....

Number of guests invited .... Number of guests who will attend.......................

Other information ....

....

....

☞ On pages 58–63
you can read more about
printed materials and how
to design an invitation.

IMPORTANT CONTACTS

	VENDOR	CONTACT PERSON	PHONE NUMBER/EMAIL
Wedding venue			
Reception hall			
Soloist			
Musician/DJ			
Catering			
Photographer			
Hairdresser			
Makeup artist			
Florist			
Bakery			

INDEX

MANY THANKS TO

*All the couples, reception halls, and
vendors who have made
this book possible.*

We would like to extend a special thanks to the following:
Florist Nyfiken Grön
Bröllopsbutiken
Face Stockholm
Chantelle
KiK
Lindex
Melanders blommor
NK Man
NK Barber shop
NK Men's shoes and accessories
Panduro Hobby
Sandberg
Stockholm Brud & Fest
Stockholm congregation
Såstaholm Hotel and Conference Center
Söders Högtidskläder
Triumph
Östermalms smoking- och frackuthyrning
Sandra Birgersdotter
Linda Broström
Hanna Jacobsson
Sofia Scheutz

Copyright © 2013 by *Allt om Bröllop* magazine

English Translation © 2014 by Skyhorse Publishing

First published in 2013 as *Allt om Bröllop* by *Allt om Bröllop* magazine, Bonnier Fakta, Sweden

Photography © 2013 Sandra Birgersdotter and Linda Broström

Illustrations © 2013 Sofia Scheutz

Illustrations on pages 132, 141, 154, 160, 187 © 2013 Anna Nilsson

Graphic design by Sofia Scheutz

Adapted for the American audience by Constance Renfrow and Bob Trehy

Skyhorse Publishing books may be purchased in bulk at special discounts for sales promotion, corporate gifts, fund-raising, or educational purposes. Special editions can also be created to specifications. For details, contact the Special Sales Department, Skyhorse Publishing, 307 West 36th Street, 11th Floor, New York, NY 10018 or info@skyhorsepublishing.com.

Skyhorse® and Skyhorse Publishing® are registered trademarks of Skyhorse Publishing, Inc.®, a Delaware corporation.

www.skyhorsepublishing.com

10 9 8 7 6 5 4 3 2 1

Library of Congress Cataloging-in-Publication Data is available on file.

Print ISBN: 978-1-62914-421-4

Ebook ISBN: 978-1-62914-931-8

Printed in China